NEW PERSPECTIVES ON THE CIVIL WAR

*Published in cooperation with
the State Historical Society of Wisconsin*

New Perspectives on the Civil War

MYTHS AND REALITIES OF THE NATIONAL CONFLICT

Edited by
John Y. Simon & Michael E. Stevens

MADISON HOUSE
Madison 1998

Simon & Stevens, ed.
New Perspectives on the Civil War
Myths and Realities of the National Conflict

Copyright © 1998 by Madison House Publishers, Inc.

LIBRARY OF CONGRESS CATALOGING-IN-PUBLICATION DATA

New perspectives on the Civil War : myths and realities of the national conflict
/ edited by John Y. Simon & Michael E. Stevens.—1st ed.
p.   cm.
Includes bibliographical references and index.
Contents: Civilized belligerents /Mark E. Neely, Jr.—Considering Lee
considered /Alan T. Nolan—Forging a commander / John Y. Simon—
Stonewall Jackson / James I. Robertson, Jr.—From Antebellum Unionist to
lost cause warrior / Gary W. Gallagher—The common soldier of the Civil
War / Joseph T. Glatthaar—Mirrors beyond memories / Ervin L. Jordan, Jr.
ISBN 0-945612-62-1 (acid-free recycled paper)
1. United States—History—Civil War, 1861–1865—Influence.
2. United States—History—Civil War, 1861–1865—Biography.
I. Simon, John Y.   II. Stevens, Michael E.
E468.9.N48 1998
973.7—dc21   98–18909

Printed in the United States of America
on acid-free recycled paper.

Published by Madison House Publishers, Inc.
P. O. Box 3100
Madison, Wisconsin 53704

FIRST EDITION

Contents

Introduction

IN HIS JANUARY 2, 1862, annual report, Lyman Copeland Draper, superintendent of the State Historical Society of Wisconsin, described the circular he had sent to Union officers asking them to "preserve for the Society, diaries of the[ir] services" in "aiding to successfully quell the wicked and unnatural rebellion of our misguided brethren of the South." Draper's appeal for historical documents soon began to bear fruit. On January 3, 1865, he reported that the Society had already collected "a vast number of statements and narratives relative to our unhappy internecine war, which will prove invaluable, and almost inexhaustible, sources of reference to the future historian of these troubled times."

More than 130 years later, Draper's prediction of ongoing interest in the Society's collections remains accurate. The Society holds more than 20,000 books, pamphlets, and other printed items and more than 750 manuscript collections and archival series dealing with the war. Researchers, including a number of the essayists in this volume, continue to use the materials that Draper and his successors collected.

The Society not only carries on the tradition through its research collections but also promotes public understanding of the latest scholarship, as evidenced by the Society's May 1995 conference on the Civil War. More than nine hundred eager participants thronged the meeting, a large and attentive audience that included teenagers as well as those old enough to be their grandparents.

Civil War programs frequently draw larger audiences than do other aspects of American history. Amateurs and professionals, scholars and students, meet on common ground. Issues raised by the war, including its causes and consequences, reverberate through contemporary society. Family and community connections with the war exist everywhere, as do battlefields, memorials, and other physical reminders of the conflict. Fascination arises from the sheer magnitude of the war, which was fought over thousands of miles of American soil and resulted in awesome casualties. It was a gigantic drama enacted by people who seem both contemporary and remote.

At least 40 million viewers watched Ken Burns's lengthy 1990 television version of the Civil War. Surging book sales and the increasing circulation of several Civil War magazines reflect invigorated popular interest in the topic. Shelby Foote's three-volume history of the war sold a respectable 30,000 copies in the fifteen years before he starred as featured narrator in Burns's series; 100,000 sets sold in the following six months. Tour operators and lecture promoters have become war profiteers. Nearly ten years later, this new interest in the Civil War shows no signs of ebbing. Perhaps the success of the television series has reflected as well as stimulated the popularity of its subject.

As the American Civil War recedes ever farther into the past, popular interest continues to rise. Once a matter that chiefly concerned veterans, separately organized North and South, who gathered to refight old battles and to memorialize the heroes and victims of war, the Civil War has gradually become part of a collective heritage. Organizations of soldiers' descendants decline, while those based on enthusiasm rather than heredity proliferate. The first of the Civil War Round Tables, organized in Chicago in 1940, has become the prototype for more than two hundred others across the United States and beyond its borders. The first of these Round Tables and almost all of its immediate progeny limited membership to men, but nearly all have now reversed this policy, some gracefully, others only after acrimonious debate.

In 1989, a fully uniformed Civil War reenactor leaving the ladies' room at the Antietam National Battlefield Park shocked park personnel. They soon learned that Lauren Cook Burgess possessed every qualification to use the ladies' room but disputed her right to appear in uniform. Such questioning led eventually to a sex discrimination suit, which Burgess won. She proclaimed her right to reenact the role of Civil War–era women who dressed as men to fight the war. Their numbers are unknown: some were detected when wounded or when giving birth; others revealed their secret only after the war; some may never have done so. Amid such uncertainty, claims that many women clandestinely enlisted cannot be refuted.

Burgess and other women join approximately 40,000 males who participate in reenacting battles, camping in the field, and presenting "living history" by dressing meticulously to impersonate soldiers. Few men care more deeply about their clothing. Some enhance their identification with the past by sewing their own uniforms and cobbling their own shoes. Many women attend reenactments costumed as contemporary wives, nurses, or widows. In August 1996 *Civil War News* reported, "Penny George is a Baltimore social worker during the week, but on weekends she portrays a prostitute with the 2nd U.S. Regulars."

During the war, many found the call to the colors irresistible. The U.S. Army recorded 127 enlistments of boys at age thirteen and 330 at fourteen; many more boys ran away from home to enlist and lied to authorities forbidden to accept such youngsters as recruits. In contrast, the 2,366 enlistees over fifty may have boasted proudly about their age. Statistics are lacking, but the Confederacy faced manpower shortages that put proportionately greater numbers of young and old in uniform. Reenactor ranks can thus appropriately hold both fathers and sons.

Some blacks found their way into Union ranks even before the federal government authorized their enlistment, and at least a few served in the Confederate army. Following the successful motion picture *Glory*, which dramatized the saga of the heroic troops of the 54th Massachusetts, more black reenactors have appeared, reinforcing the ranks of those already uniformed to perform for themselves and any audience they could attract. If many Civil War reenactors seem too old, too fat, and too happy to do justice to the boys who fought, the producers of the movie *Gettysburg* could not reject the thousands of volunteers who appeared already costumed and equipped for virtually uncompensated service in that mammoth commercial reenactment. In reaction to such enthusiasm, some historians have become concerned that recreational and entertainment aspects of the Civil War might obscure its serious interpretation.

While the Civil War has become everyone's war, scholarly interest is shifting to new aspects of the conflict. Perennial concerns with battles, leaders, strategy, and tactics are being supplemented by new attention to the experience of common soldiers and the impact of the war behind the lines. Long exempt from the scrutiny of social historians, the era is now providing bountiful sources with which to investigate the careers and culture of ordinary people. Some historians reappraise the prevailing consensus on political and military topics, while others explore new subjects.

In 1990 the deputy executive director of the American Historical Association, a leading professional organization, testified against a proposed Civil War Sites Advisory Commission because the legislation assumed that battlefields held "special historical significance" based upon "emotional appeal." He believed that the "traditional preoccupation with wars and presidents" represented "narrow, antiquated views of the past." Instead, he urged the federal government to "respond to the challenging new topics and perspectives of modern scholarship."

The controversy over battlefield preservation demonstrates the enduring vitality of those "antiquated" issues as well as others (sometimes mistakenly) believed to be new and innovative. The public denounces the growing urban sprawl of Washington, D.C., when suburbia and commercial development threaten to engulf hallowed ground where men fought and died. Battlefield preservation and historical commemoration have become matters of public interest. Many conflicting voices advocate recognition of neglected aspects of the war. Forgotten or traduced leaders find latter-day advocates: at least three groups have formed to commemorate Confederate General James Longstreet.

THE PRESENTATIONS at the conference, aimed at a popular audience and revised for this volume, reflect the vitality and diversity of thinking on the war. They range from Mark Neely's rejection of "total war" theorists to James I. Robertson's disagreement with Ken Burns's characterization of Stonewall Jackson; from Ervin Jordan's recollection of his youthful astonishment in learning about the existence of black soldiers in the Civil War to Alan Nolan's discussion of the persistence of the Lost Cause. Together, the essays confront some of the conventional wisdom and myths that have developed around the war.

Pulitzer Prize–winner Mark E. Neely, Jr., opens the book with an essay about Abraham Lincoln and the concept of total war. Neely examines the arguments of total-war theorists, who suggest that the North waged war on people and paralyzed the Confederacy's economic capacity. He maintains that the economic explanation gained favor in the twentieth century because it offered a reason for the South's defeat that did not require the acknowledgment of any moral failings on the part of the Confederacy. Neely tests the theory against Lincoln's beliefs and argues that the president did not deviate from the Victorian code of warfare against "civilized belligerents"—other white men of European ancestry. Thus, the concept of the Civil War as total war did not arise from historical evidence but rather from the intellectual climate created by Allied tactics in World War II.

Alan T. Nolan revisits the image of Robert E. Lee and the "Lost Cause." Nolan examines the development of the Lost Cause mythology, which saw the conflict as "essentially romantic, a contest of honor and martial glory in which brave and valorous men and women contended over the issue of Southern independence." The Lost Cause legend discounted slavery as a cause of the war, played up cultural differences between the North and the South, and blamed military defeat solely on General James Longstreet's performance at Gettysburg. Nolan argues that the need to rationalize the war in social terms and northern racism contributed to the creation of the Lost Cause ideology and to Lee's elevation to the status of Warrior Hero, a canonization that required the distortion of the general's views. Nolan's 1991 book, *Lee Considered*, challenged some of these misrepresentations, and he responds to some of the criticism it has received. In the end, Nolan insists that if history is to replace legend, Lee must be seen as a "historical character of human proportions," with attendant flaws.

John Y. Simon examines the rapid rise of Ulysses S. Grant to command in the first year of the Civil War. The war disrupted traditional practices in the army's seniority system. Because of their advanced age, many high-ranking prewar officers could not effectively command troops in battle, a situation that provided opportunities for younger field commanders. Grant's comparatively young age, combined with his ambivalence toward military orthodoxy, contributed to his amazing self-assurance and audacity. Although younger than Grant, George B. McClellan had the dual responsibilities of protecting the nation's capital and engaging the enemy army, leaving him no opportunity to experiment or to learn through error. Good fortune alone did not explain Grant's success, for he seized military opportunities and responded effectively to adversity. Within one year after leaving a clerkship in a provincial town, Grant had exhibited generalship essential to Northern victory.

James I. Robertson, Jr., rejects Ken Burns's description in the PBS *Civil War* television series of Stonewall Jackson as a "pious, blue-eyed killer." Robertson notes Jackson's complexity, characterizing him as a superb military leader who displayed courage under fire and exhibited concern for his men's welfare. Because Jackson died halfway through the Civil War, at the pinnacle of his career, he remains unencumbered by the weight of the South's defeat: one can speculate about how his military skills might have aided the Confederacy and changed the course of the war. That

speculation, combined with Jackson's charisma, "a divinely inspired gift that captures the popular imagination and inspires allegiance and devotion," creates the heroic image of Jackson that
endures today.

Gary W. Gallagher discusses the odyssey of Jubal A. Early, who
opposed Virginia's secession from the Union in 1861 but by 1867
went into self-imposed exile in Canada to escape "Yankee rule."
Gallagher argues that what seems to be a radical change in ideology
was in reality steadfast devotion to the same basic conservative principles. Just as Early opposed the dissolution of the prewar Union, he
also resisted the radical changes enacted by the U.S. government
during and after the war—especially emancipation and what he
viewed as outrages against Confederate civilians and their property.
Whereas other southerners adapted in the postwar era, "Early clung
doggedly to his beliefs in the Constitution as it had been, the correctness of slavery, rule by a propertied elite, and the need for white
supremacy in a biracial society."

Joseph T. Glatthaar focuses on the more than three million common soldiers of the Confederate and Union armies, whose experiences
represented a radical change from their prewar lives. Glatthaar describes the backgrounds of those who served, discusses why they
fought, and illuminates the conditions they faced. Drawing heavily
from soldiers' letters home, he describes weaponry, training and living conditions, relations between soldiers and their officers, entertainment, letter writing, and morality. He also recounts other aspects of
soldiers' lives, including food, clothing, health and medicine, fear, and
the horror of combat. Glatthaar vividly brings out the human side of
the war, making the participants and their struggles come alive.

African Americans have often been forgotten participants in
the Civil War, although in recent years historians have attempted
to make amends. Ervin L. Jordan, Jr., discusses how an interest in
his own heritage led him to explore the role of Virginia's blacks in
the war. Virginia was home to one of every six blacks living in the
Confederacy, most but not all of them slaves. Jordan examines a
number of topics, including religion, punishment, and slave resis-

tance. He pays special attention to black women, noting their active opposition to the Confederate war effort, the sexual violence they suffered, and the interracial marriages they contracted. Jordan also discusses the few blacks who supported the Confederacy and the reprisals they faced from other Afro-Virginians, a topic that has previously received little attention.

Together, these essays offer fresh perspectives on a war that continues to haunt America, and they add to the "invaluable, and almost inexhaustible, sources of reference to the future historian" that Lyman Draper began collecting more than a century and a quarter ago.

THIS VOLUME has come into being as a result of the hard work of many people. Betsy Torrison of the State Historical Society of Wisconsin spent countless hours planning and organizing the 1995 conference, and its success resulted largely from her tireless work. Connie Beam, Matt Blessing, Edward Coffman, Dee Ducklow, Tom Howe, John Kaminski, Connie Meier, and Richard Zeitlin also substantially contributed to the conference. Former Society director Nick Muller and Associate Director Bob Thomasgard offered their support for the entire project. Ellen Goldlust-Gingrich of the Society lent her fine editorial hand to the production of the book manuscript and improved it in innumerable ways. Sue Dotson of the Ulysses S. Grant Association also furnished indispensable assistance in the preparation of the book. We are grateful to all of these people for their efforts.

John Y. Simon
Michael E. Stevens

New Perspectives on the Civil War

President Lincoln and General George B. McClellan in the general's tent, Antietam, Maryland. Courtesy Library of Congress.

"Civilized Belligerents": Abraham Lincoln and the Idea of "Total War"

Mark E. Neely, Jr.

IT WAS AN UNFORTUNATE trick of fate that this century's most fruitful period of writing on the American Civil War came only sixteen years after the United States and its allies won the greatest war in modern history by striking new methods. The strenuous mobilization of national economies, the exploitation of population superiority, saturation bombing, the infliction of more civilian casualties than military ones, and eventually the use of the atomic bomb made a deep impression on modern minds. The accident of timing—that the Civil War centennial came so near the end of World War II—proved crucial for interpretations of the American Civil War. It gave rise to the "total war" thesis, which suggested that the North won the Civil War because of its superior economic resources and population numbers, by making war on peoples rather than exclusively on armies, and by paralyzing the Confederacy's economic capacity to wage war as well as its morale.[1]

Economic History and the American Civil War

To the total-war paradigm created in the shadow of World War II we owe the obligatory first chapter of the typical modern Civil War book, a familiar litany describing Northern superiority in population (military manpower as much as 4.5:1), railroad miles (3:1), and manufacturing capacity (according to the 1860 census, the value of manufactured goods produced annually by New York state alone was four times greater than that of the eleven states that would form the Confederacy).[2]

It seems clear now, as perhaps it could not have in the shadow of World War II, that the gross disparities in manufacturing capacity between the two belligerents prove only that manufacturing was of minor importance in wars fought in the middle of the nineteenth century, for the Confederacy performed well and lasted four years despite its disadvantage. The idea of total war is post-Keynesean in economics and thus a Civil War anachronism. Government planning and direction of economic mobilization for war were not likely to occur to a nineteenth-century capitalist like Abraham Lincoln. Indeed, Congress in January 1862 gave the president authority to seize and operate any or all railroads "when in his judgment the public safety may require it," but Lincoln and the War Department in fact seldom did so. In our century, by contrast, President Woodrow Wilson, calling World War I "a war of resources no less than of men, perhaps even more than of men," seized the railroads and put his son-in-law in charge of the government board that operated them.[3]

Republicans in Congress in the 1860s had no more idea of a war of resources than the Republican president did. The program enacted by Congress during the war—raising tariffs on four occasions to as much as double their prewar levels, aiding the Pacific railroad, creating greenbacks as legal tender, altering the nature of banks, passing the Homestead Act, and funding agricultural and mechanical colleges—carried out the promises of the prewar Republican platform. Congress capitalized on the golden political opportunity created by the departure of the obstructionist southern Democrats during the war. The legislation was not primarily dictated by military considerations: homesteads and colleges, for example, competed with military recruitment and scattered men to the west instead of funneling them into the army to go south.[4]

Industrial capacity did not seem as important to Lincoln and the Republican Congress as it seemed to the historians of the Civil War writing a hundred years later in the shadow of a "total war," a "GNP war" like World War II. And industry seemed perhaps even less important to the military men in the 1860s who actually fought the war. As Gerald Linderman has suggested, soldiers looked mainly for courage, and, as Michael C. C. Adams has shown, military prowess in the Civil War era was often associated with a rural lifestyle and considered incompatible with urban and industrial society. Planters' sons could reputedly ride and shoot, and the North's pale shopkeepers seemed perhaps unequal to them in habits of command, in familiarity with firearms and violence, and in sheer stamina. Both the Southerners, who typically thought any Confederate could whip ten Yankees, and the Yankees themselves after Bull Run thought so. It was pure myth, of course, but a powerful one. Thus, South Carolina diarist Mary Chesnut offered a version of the myth in quoting Virginian Winfield Scott on the virtues and vices of the Southern soldier: "We have elan, courage, woodcraft, consummate horsemanship, endurance of pain equal to the Indians, but . . . we will not submit to discipline. We will not take care of things or husband our resources."[5]

The North's advantage in resources, impressive to Southerners at the time, did not seem particularly important to historians of the Civil War until well into the twentieth century. Early on, the focus in explaining how the North won the war lay on nonindustrial factors, primarily population and moral differences. Horace Greeley, for example, listed fourteen Northern advantages in his *American Conflict,* the subtitle of which announced the book's intention to study the war in its "moral and political phases." Among the fourteen, listed as but a small part of the population factor, he mentioned, "In Manufactures, Commerce, Shipping, etc., the preponderance was immensely on the side of the Union."[6]

It did not occur to anyone to write an economic history of the Civil War emphasizing manufacturing, organization, and management until the twentieth century. Before that time, works on wartime economic questions focused mostly on the financing of the Northern war effort, especially the Legal Tender Act creating paper currency, or greenbacks. Questions of hard versus soft money were as hot as any political topic in the late nineteenth century, and such works were not really economic history but shots fired in the contemporary political battles over gold, silver, and paper currency.[7] Not even as obvious a topic as Civil War railroads gained the attention of historians before the twentieth century. The earliest book on the influence of railroads on the war came in 1916 and was the work of a British historian impressed with their uses in mobilization for World War I.[8]

The impulse to write about the economic history of the Civil War came from twentieth-century academia, not from participants in the conflict, many of whom were still alive and writing as America entered the new century. A revealing moment in the changing interpretations of the war came in 1905, when Wisconsin established a commission to memorialize that state's part in the war for the upcoming fiftieth anniversary in 1911. The commission's professional intellectuals outnumbered its military veteran element. A professor of history at the University of Wisconsin, the secretary of the State Historical Society, the secretary of the Wisconsin Free Library Commission, and one GAR member formed the commission. From this group emerged a "scholar's plan" recommending "a widening of the scope of the initial act," and the result was one of the earliest economic histories of the war, Frederick Merk's *Economic History of Wisconsin during the Civil War Decade,* published in 1916. Merk sneered at the original commission's idea that the projected historical works should describe "the part played by Wisconsin soldiers in the war, of which every citizen of the state was believed to be 'justly proud.'"

At the university in those days professors were developing a different kind of history from the old flag-and-drum military history. Merk, therefore, wrote about logging, brewing, railroads, mortgages, and the origins of government regulation of railroads in the 1860s—the whole decade, incidentally—and merely tacked on the conclusion that "the North succeeded in 1865 in restoring the Union and destroying slavery not because its people were more patriotic, its soldiers braver, or its generals more skillful than those of the South. Victory . . . rested with the side that could bring to bear the weight of superior resources." [9]

The first economic study of the war slightly preceded Merk's book—Emerson D. Fite's *Social and Industrial Conditions in the North during the Civil War* (1910). Encouraged by his professors at Harvard and his colleagues at Yale, Fite sought to prove that "war and politics were" not "the only topics which then held the attention of the people." In other words, he revealed the persistence of normal economic life, including vast indulgence in "luxuries and amusements" while the war went on. Thus, of "public improvements," Fite concluded, "proceeding in the time of prolonged war, the signs of municipal progress . . . are of especial significance; they were the same as in normal times, and they give a peculiar emphasis to the fact that local interests were not swallowed up in national interests, and that municipal development and municipal pride, as well as war, politics, and business, claimed a share of public attention." Fite said that "the spirit of commerce proved to be consistent with the spirit of war." The idea that economic development could occur during war and not be stifled by it—as peace advocates charged in Fite's day— summed up the point of the first generation of economic histories of the American Civil War. Fite did not see the North's vital economy as linked to the success of the war effort but rather as proof that conflict did not absorb the country's total energies, the opposite of what "total war" theorists would later imply.[10]

The earliest origins of the economic proposition embodied in the "total war" idea came not from northern historians writing in the twentieth century but from Southern generals and politicians immediately after the Civil War. The defeated Southerners wanted some excuse for their failure to win the war, and an emphasis on Northern superiority in numbers and resources loomed most important in southern explanations of defeat from Appomattox until well into the twentieth century. Robert E. Lee may have hit on the idea as early as anyone when he said in his farewell to the Army of Northern Virginia that "the Army . . . has been compelled to yield to overwhelming numbers and resources."[11] This excuse has always seemed attractive in Lost Cause mythology, for it meant that southerners did not have to acknowledge any moral failings—there was nothing wrong with the cause, and the spirit of the allegedly solid South was willing. In the end, emphasis on economic factors in Confederate defeat would meet little sectional resistance: it was the sort of idea on which northern and southern historians might agree.

World War II and the Interpretation of the American Civil War

From southerners, too, came the earliest and most persistent allegations that the North engaged in the practices associated in the twentieth century with the concept of "total war": waging war on innocent civilians and on women and children and deliberately destroying private property. Politicians and generals indulged in this rhetoric to whip up hatred for the enemy during the war. Jefferson Davis began making such accusations about the Union war effort even before the first Battle of Bull Run, and he continued making them to the bitter end.

After World War II, northern historians began to agree with Davis that the North waged war by atrocity. It surely constitutes one of the strangest intellectual migrations of modern historiography, producing a truly nonsectional explanation of Union victory: the total-war theory. Explaining the northern historians' willing consent to this thesis is not easy, but World War II may lie at the root of it.

The aftermath of the Second World War lacked the turning away from war on the part of intellectuals that had marked the post–World War I era. Instead, because the goals of the war had been clearer and because the cold war ensued immediately, there was a retention, even among liberal intellectuals, of the hard-boiled attitudes common during any war.[12] One result was that the intellectual style of the post–World War II period was distinctly realistic. Tough-mindedness was as high praise as an intellectual could receive or bestow upon another intellectual. And swearing—as Paul Fussell has shown in *Wartime: Understanding and Behavior in the Second World War* (1989)—became one of the most vivid legacies of World War II. Profanity seemed the only authentic voice in a war sold to the public by the euphemisms of public relations and government propaganda and by the corrupt superlatives of advertising.[13] Thus, it helped William T. Sherman's reputation substantially that he said—or was widely believed to have said—"War is hell." Post–World War II historians admired that style.

As Michael Sherry points out in *In the Shadow of War: The United States since the 1930s,* the idea of "total war" was much in the atmosphere. "Total war," said Conyers Read, the head of the American Historical Association, in his 1949 presidential address, "whether it be hot or cold, enlists everyone and calls upon everyone to assume his part. The historian is no freer from this obligation than the physicist."[14] The effect of World War II on writing about the American Civil War was quick and dramatic. The hard-nosed approach immediately created an atmosphere sympathetic to the brutal notions embodied in the idea of "total war," now stripped of their previous taint of brutality by Allied victory through economic mobilization, saturation bombing, and atomic warfare. The landmark attacks on the prewar interpretations of the Civil War, which came from Bernard DeVoto in *Harper's Magazine* in 1946 and from Arthur M. Schlesinger, Jr., in *Partisan Review* in 1949, criticized earlier historians for sentimentalism. Indeed, the title of Schlesinger's influential article was "The Causes of the Civil War: A Note on Historical Sentimentalism." The new outlook on the war was more tough minded.[15]

The antisentimental outlook left its mark on perhaps the most influential book on the war written since World War II, *Why the North Won the Civil War,* edited by David Donald and offering different interpretations by Donald, Richard N. Current, T. Harry Williams, David Potter, and Norman A. Graebner. Because of its compact size, able writing, and variety of theories, the book has been widely assigned in college courses, quietly spreading the "total war" outlook on the American Civil War. The military historian among the authors, T. Harry Williams, who had become the generation's most important interpreter of Lincoln as commander in chief with the publication of *Lincoln and His Generals* in 1952, expressed the officers' mess-room toughness and the secure gender assumptions taken over by male intellectuals after World War II. Setting up a contrast between "total war" and its predecessor in the Age of Reason, Williams wrote that eighteenth-century warfare "was conducted with a measure of humanity that caused Chesterfield to say: 'War is pusillanimously carried on in this degenerate age: quarter is given; towns are taken and people spared; even in a storm, a woman can hardly hope for the benefit of a rape.'" By contrast, Williams went on, Lincoln, in the nineteenth century, needed generals who realized war "was bound to be a rough no-holds-barred affair, a bloody and brutal struggle."[16]

The book's essay on Civil War diplomacy, written by Graebner, scorned "idealism" in foreign policy and celebrated "realpolitik," a term used twice in the article. "Realities of power," not "sentimentalism and faith in moral pressure," were thought determinative in international affairs. And Donald began his essay on the morale and character of the opposing armies by noting that historians attribute "to the victor [in war] the masculine traits of strength, power, aggressiveness, and tough-mindedness."[17]

The cumulative effect of this language and outlook was what might be called a cult of fierceness in interpreting Northern victory in the Civil War. By 1986 historian James McPherson wrote that President Lincoln, realizing the true nature of total war, "sanctioned this policy of 'being terrible' on the enemy."[18] Charles Royster, in *The Destructive War: William Tecumseh Sherman, Stonewall Jackson, and the Americans,* voiced the cult of fierceness in its most overwrought extreme, writing that the Northern and Southern

> experience of war was partly a flight into unreason: into visions of purgation and redemption, into anticipation and intuition and spiritual apotheosis, into bloodshed that was not only intentional pursuit of interests of state but was also sacramental, erotic, mystical and strangely gratifying. This process of taking the war to heart, believ-

ing that it would change everyone, worked as strongly as any other influence toward making it more inclusive and more destructive.

Among Northerners, Abraham Lincoln made himself the pre-eminent example of the noncombatant united to the war seeming to draw into himself the pain of its destructiveness.[19]

When the preoccupations of the civil rights struggle edged out the cold war assumptions of post–World War II historians, the emphasis in the "total war" theory changed from the "bloody and brutal" warfare depicted by Williams to the "terrible" war of McPherson or Royster that was thought to have the ability to "change everyone." Historians now seized on the element of social revolutionary change necessarily wrought in an enemy society devastated by total war. The "total war" thesis proved well adapted to the idea of a civil war that destroyed southern social institutions and left possibilities of entirely reconstructing southern society. In short, "total war" was subtly transformed from an idea of war in which the North gained victory by ceasing to distinguish between combatants and noncombatants to an idea of war in which the North's policy goal was to revolutionize slave society. Thus, McPherson said that the North at first fought "to suppress th[e] insurrection and restore loyal Unionists to control of the southern states. The conflict was therefore a limited war . . . with the limited goal of restoring the status quo ante bellum, not an unlimited war to destroy an enemy nation and re-shape its society." There is a difference between a war with a goal of reshaping a society and a war in which killing civilians is a legitimate means of combat, but the two ideas became quietly confused. Eric Foner, who writes mainly on Reconstruction rather than on the war itself, easily took over the idea, writing, for example, "In December 1861, Lincoln had admonished Congress that the Civil War must not degenerate into a 'violent and remorseless revolutionary struggle.' The Emancipation Proclamation announced that this was precisely what it must become." Echoing McPherson, Foner said that "no aspect of life emerged untouched from the conflict."[20]

Of course, no historian argued, as Jefferson Davis had, that the North had waged "total war" from the very start: historians thought that the North moved from limited war in 1861 to total war by 1864, and the application of that new doctrine by Lincoln, Ulysses S. Grant, Sherman, and Philip Sheridan brought victory to the North and a revolution in southern social institutions. In other words, the war, following a dynamic of violence pointed out by military theorist Carl von Clausewitz, became less limited as time went on. But whatever its imagined chronological dynamic or its qualification as an ideal type, the idea of "total war" remains flatly inapplicable to the Civil War and utterly distorts its carefully controlled nature. [21]

Abraham Lincoln and the Concept of Total War

The case for "total war" has always been suspiciously short of documentation proving that any such policy of deliberate fierceness toward southern civilians was a conscious policy of the Lincoln administration. The theory's champions could readily enough quote Abraham Lincoln's early statements of what he did not want the war to be, but they could not come up with any statement showing that he changed his mind and embraced the opposite view. The most important reason that no such evidence could be found is that Lincoln never changed his mind on the treatment of noncombatants. Another reason is that Lincoln was commander in chief and not a theoretician of warfare. He waged war, but he rarely discussed it in the abstract. Discerning his concept of war requires scouring his correspondence and speeches for the occasional revealing passage. But when it is done, it becomes clear that Lincoln, far from conceiving some new and terrible idea of war, clearly stated his adherence to a traditional Victorian conception of war.

The relevant documents are those written from 1863 through 1865. The timing of the alleged transformation from limited to "total war" has always been vague, but most advocates of the theory seem to agree that it came after January 1, 1863. From that period to the end of his life, I have found three Lincoln documents that bear directly on the ideas embraced in the concept of "total war." The first is the famous Conkling letter, which formed the Republican platform for the state and local elections of 1863. The point of the document, written to be read aloud at a political rally in Illinois and spread in printed form later, was to defend the Emancipation Proclamation as fully legal within the traditional restraints of warfare: "Is there— has there ever been—any questions that by the law of war, property, both of enemies and friends, may be taken when needed? And is it not needed whenever taking it, helps us, or hurts the enemy? Armies, the world over, destroy enemies' property when they can not use it; and even destroy their own to keep it from the enemy. Civilized belligerents do all in their power to help themselves, or hurt the enemy, except a few things regarded as barbarous or cruel. Among the exceptions are the massacre of vanquished foes, and non-combatants, male and female."[22] The Emancipation Proclamation, in other words, was as far as Lincoln would go to extend the reach of warfare. Having done it, he remained secure in his belief that the accepted boundaries of legitimate warfare stood untouched and unquestionable by civilized people. He never thought otherwise.

The second document, though less revealing in a way, does deal directly with southern white civilians and Sherman's policies toward them. But the civilians in question were probably East Tennesseans, who had long owned a martyr status in northern minds. In the spring 1864, Sherman's camps in Tennessee were thronged with refugees, and in exasperation he published a general order "to citizens at military posts south of Nashville. When citizens cannot procure provisions in the country there is no alternative but they must remove to the rear. . . . It is idle for us to be pushing forward subsistence stores if they are lavished and expended on any persons except . . . the army proper." Someone protested to the president, and on May 4, 1864, he wrote to Sherman, "I have an imploring appeal in behalf of the citizens who say your order No. 8 will compel them to go North of Nashville. This is in no sense, an order; nor is it even a request; that you will do any thing which in the least, shall be a drawback upon your military operations, but any thing you can do consistently with those operations, for those suffering people, I shall be glad of." Lincoln knew of Sherman's diabolical hatred of politicians and of any interference with military operations; the president wrote to the general gingerly. Even so, Sherman refused to change his order. He asserted again that "the railroad cannot supply the army & the people too." He dismissed the Tennesseans' protest as largely a "humbug" but relented enough to promise, "We can relieve all actual suffering by each company or regiment giving of their savings. Every man who is willing to fight and work gets all rations & all who won't fight or work should go away and we offer them free transportation."[23]

Two points seem clear from this exchange. First, as late as the spring 1864, Lincoln had no policy toward southern civilians, let alone one of treating them terribly. One balance, if military operations were not compromised, his impulse was to alleviate civilian suffering. Second, Sherman, though allegedly the architect of "total war," apparently had no policy on the question either; at least he did not defend his order by saying that some enemy citizens should be made to feel war's hardships.

A third document, written about a year after the Conkling letter, deals with the destruction of private property in the South. It is a telegram, in cipher, sent to General Grant, also allegedly a proponent of "total war," on August 14, 1864: "The Secretary of War and I concur that you better confer with Gen. Lee and stipulate for a mutual discontinuance of house-burning and other destruction of private property. The time and manner of conference, and particulars of stipulation we leave, on our part, to your convenience and judgment." Grant refused, saying that experience had taught him "that agreements made with rebels are binding upon us but are not observed by them longer than suits their convenience." He thought the best that could be done under the circumstances was to "publish a prohibitory order against burning private property except where it is a Military necessity or in retaliation for like acts by the enemy."[24]

Once again, it is notable that Grant commented only on the mechanism for bringing about the end desired by the commander in chief: he did not tell the president that burning and destruction of private property of rebels was his strategy for winning the war because it was not. And in this instance, it is important to understand what particular abuses were under discussion. An examination of the surviving mail written to the White House reveals no immediate provocation called to Lincoln's attention in the first two weeks of August. The letter surely refers to the events fresh and vivid in everyone's memory in the eastern theater that summer, the burning of Chambersburg, Pennsylvania, by Jubal Early's cavalry on July 30, 1864.

Lincoln and Secretary of War Edwin M. Stanton had talked of mutual cessation of house burning because they knew that General Early had attacked Chambersburg as retaliation for Union general David Hunter's depredations in the Shenandoah Valley from the burning of the Virginia Military Institute in Lexington on June 11, 1864, to the destruction of Virginia Governor John Letcher's house in July. By midsummer Hunter had been acting under a set of Grant's orders, now famous, that directed (as communicated by Henry W. Halleck) that if Hunter could not cut railroads around Charlottesville, Virginia, "he should make all the valleys south of the Baltimore and Ohio road a desert as high up as possible." "I do not mean that houses should be burned," Grant stipulated, "but every particle of provisions and stock should be removed, and the people notified to move out." The general wanted Hunter's "troops to eat out Virginia clear and clean as far as they go, so that crows flying over it for the balance of the season will have to carry their provender with them."[25]

Although Grant's orders had specifically ruled out burning private houses, it nevertheless became an issue. Early had likewise given orders against "making war on the defenseless and unresisting" when his army invaded the North, but reports from Chambersburg mentioned specifically and prominently the house-burning issue. The earliest Union report, from William W. Averell to Darius N. Couch in Harrisburg, Pennsylvania, stated that Confederates had "set fire to the principal portion of Chambersburg," that "some provision should be made for the citizens whose houses have been burned," and that "it was the intention of the enemy to burn Carlisle also, in retaliation for the burning of private houses by General Hunter." About three weeks earlier Secretary of the Navy Gideon Welles had read in the newspapers Governor Letcher's charge that "General

Hunter gave the order for burning his (L.'s) house." Welles suspended judgment for the time being, but he knew Hunter lacked "prudence." He concluded that "indiscriminate warfare on all in the insurrectionary region is not general, and few would destroy private property wantonly." Lincoln and Stanton evidently shared Welles's opinion on that question.[26]

Hunter was replaced for various reasons by August 8, and the letter to Grant followed but six days later. Such activities as Hunter's and Early's are examples of the harsh practices usually associated with "total war," and Lincoln, Stanton, and Welles clearly opposed them.

There does not exist a single Lincoln document, hardly a sentence or fragment in his handwriting, that articulated a policy of "total war" or endorsed any of the ruthless practices associated with it. Instead, there are only instances of disapproval of such practices. Lincoln much preferred to see the suffering of civilians relieved. He did not approve of the burning of private property. Is it any wonder that the vogue of "total war" theory is on the decline in Civil War studies? Historians now avoid using the term, if not the concept, and the concept has developed a relentless critic in Eric T. Dean of Yale. Mark Grimsley has also carefully studied and characterized the evolution of Union military policy toward southern civilians in ways that escape the "total war" paradigm of interpretation.[27]

The Problem of the Indian Wars

Interpretive paradigms cannot be contained within the periods or fields of their origin; they inevitably bleed into other areas. Thus, histories of warfare against the Plains Indians after the Civil War are now replete with references to "total war." Western historians posit a "continuity in tactics and strategy between the Civil War and the frontier wars," arguing that the successful Civil War practitioners of "systematic warfare against civilians"—Grant, Sherman, and Sheridan—directed wars aimed at "subjugating entire races of people in the West."[28] In 1967 Robert M. Utley called the attention of other historians of the Indian wars to "the growing practice of 'total war'" that he saw developing on the frontier toward 1865. "Sherman and Sheridan," he said, "who applied the technique in Georgia and Virginia during the Civil War, would give it further significance in the postwar years."[29] When in later research Utley investigated the Plains Indian wars of the late nineteenth century, he characterized U.S. Army strategy as "total war": "In engagement after engagement, women and children fell victim to army bullets or were cast upon a hostile country, often in winter, without food or shelter." Though many officers disavowed killing women and children, Utley concluded, "The significant point is that Sherman's strategy for the conquest of the Indians was as moral, or immoral, as his march across Georgia in the Civil War or as more recent military actions involving civilian populations." In an oft-quoted passage, Utley concluded, "Sherman and Sheridan were of a single mind on strategy. Atlanta and the Shenandoah Valley furnished the precedents. Like Georgians and Virginians four years earlier, the Cheyennes and Arapahoes would suffer total war."[30] The idea is still current in military histories of the period of the Indian wars. Thus in *Crossing the Deadly Ground: United States Army Tactics, 1865–1899*, published in 1994, Perry Jamieson entitles his chapter on tactics and strategy in the Indian wars "The Same Principle as at Atlanta."[31]

But as Michael Fellman has pointed out, what is remarkable is not the similarity but the dissimilarity of the nature of war waged by white men against each other and by white men against people perceived as other races.[32] Although Victorians waged vicious warfare against those who were deemed savages, they never did so against what Lincoln called "civilized belligerents"—other white men of European ancestry. The United States did not hang Confederate prisoners of war as it attempted to hang more than three hundred Sioux Indians after the Minnesota uprising in 1862, and it did not dispossess the Confederates of the land on which they lived, as it did the tribes that rebelled in Minnesota. The direct contrast between the treatment accorded the Sioux in the 1862 uprising and the Confederates warring against the United States at exactly the same moment constitutes grim proof that "total war" was not the way the Union and Confederacy fought each other. It was reserved only for groups perceived as other races.

On this score, Abraham Lincoln revealed himself to be more humane than many of his Victorian peers. After a military commission in Minnesota sentenced 303 Sioux to death for "participation in . . . murders and outrages," Lincoln discussed the event in his cabinet, directed the general in charge (H. H. Sibley) to hang no one without sanction, demanded the trial records, and then had them examined with an eye to distinguishing those Indians found guilty of rape or murder from those who had fought in pitched battles with white soldiers. In the end, he allowed thirty-eight to hang and pardoned the others. They remained prisoners of the government and were removed from Minnesota with the rest of the Sioux.

Just as the army's double standard for dealing with Indians and white belligerents reveals the limits of civilized Victorian warfare, so too Lincoln's personal involvement in the aftermath of the Sioux uprising illustrates his outlook on warfare. Lincoln held no particularly strong or enlightened views on Indians. His grandfather had been murdered by them, which deprived Lincoln's father of education and of the opportunity to make something of himself. Lincoln did not admire his father, and, ultimately, his father's shortcomings could be blamed on Indians. When an Indian war broke out in Illinois in 1831, Lincoln was quick to enlist, but he saw no hostile Indians and apparently protected a friendly one from the unthinking vengeance of other whites. When, as president, Lincoln met with Indian delegations in Washington, he spoke to them in ridiculous pidgin English and lectured them from stereotyped assumptions: they were too warlike, they were primitive hunters and gatherers, and they needed to adopt agriculture.[33]

But about warfare Lincoln had ingrained convictions. He did not think that "vanquished foes" should be "massacred"; civilized belligerents did not do so. The laws of war treated as criminals undisciplined murderers and rapists but not men who fought in battle with organized forces. Lincoln also applied this code, perhaps stretching the Victorian attitude toward race, to American Indians.

Lincoln's Character Emerges
from the Shadow of Total War

Lincoln did not search for generals to make war more "brutal." He did not want to be "terrible" on the enemy because he did not desire a legacy of hatred and revenge in the South. Before the war, unlike almost all other Republicans, as David Donald points out, Lincoln never indulged in attacks on the bogeyman the Republicans called the Slave Power—the 1 percent of Americans who held many slaves and allegedly conspired to nationalize slavery and spread it across the North as well as the South and West. Lincoln accused Democratic politicians but not southerners of seeking that end. He simply did not hate southerners as most Republicans did.[34]

Toward southerners Lincoln was singularly nonvindictive from the beginning of the war to what he hoped would be its ending without malice. Historians revising the sentimental image of the mythical Lincoln after World War II, or revising the history of Reconstruction during the civil rights era, went too far when they revised sentiment out of Lincoln's policies. The classic instance of the postwar desentimentalization was the essay on Lincoln that appeared in Edmund Wilson's *Patriotic Gore: Studies in the Literature of the American Civil War* (1962). After introducing the volume by comparing Lincoln to Bismarck and Lenin, Wilson attacked Carl Sandburg. "There are moments," Wilson wrote in an oft-quoted passage, "when one is tempted to feel that the cruellest thing that has happened to Lincoln since he was shot by Booth has been to fall into the hands of Carl Sandburg." Wilson concluded, "The amorphous and coarse-meshed Sandburg is incapable of doing justice to the tautness and the hard distinction that we find when, disregarding legends, we attack Lincoln's writings in bulk. These writings do not give the impression of a folksy and jocular countryman swapping yarns at the village store or making his way to the White House by uncertain and awkward steps or presiding like a father, with a tear in his eye, over the tragedy of the Civil War."[35]

Most historians still agree that Sandburg's bucolic legends richly merit banishment from Lincoln biography, but the baby should not be thrown out with the bath water. Lincoln was by no stretch of the imagination a Bismarck. There must be some room for sentiment in modern portraits of Lincoln. It does not capture the man to use the language of "realpolitik" or terms like *hard, terrible, brutal,* or *remorseless.*

Lincoln's legacy in warfare was civilization and restraint. He did not wage no-holds-barred, brutal, terrible, remorseless, or bloody war as a matter of conscious policy in preference to the civilized limits most nineteenth-century policymakers assumed would be applied in organized warfare. Historians who thought they saw such developments in Lincoln's war in fact had their judgment obscured by the great shadow of World War II. Later, the perception of a revolution in race policy refueled the tendency to see in Lincoln's policies toward the white South a destructiveness that was not really present. Lincoln never encouraged brutality in war, and he never linked liberation with destruction.

Notes

1. See Richard Pells, *The Liberal Mind in a Conservative Age: American Intellectuals in the 1940s and 1950s,* 2d ed. (Middletown, Ct.: Wesleyan University Press, 1989), esp. 40–51, for civilian losses as the most significant quality of World War II.

2. Phillip S. Paludan, *"A People's Contest": The Union and the Civil War, 1861–1865* (New York: Harper and Row, 1988), 105, provides the remarkable manufacturing statistic.

3. Thomas Weber, *The Northern Railroads in the Civil War, 1861–1865* (New York: King's Crown Press, 1952), 99, 105, 15, 27, 43; Mark E. Neely, Jr., *The Last Best Hope of Earth: Abraham Lincoln and the Promise of America* (Cambridge: Harvard University Press, 1994), 138. An underestimated factor in Southern resilience was the minor economic miracle wrought by Jefferson Davis, the War Department, and the Confederate Congress. See Emory M. Thomas, *The Confederacy as a Revolutionary Experience* (Englewood Cliffs, N.J.: Prentice-Hall, 1971), esp. 79–99.

4. J. Matthew Gallman, *The North Fights the Civil War: The Home Front* (Chicago: Ivan R. Dee, 1994), esp. 92–103.

5. Gerald F. Linderman, *Embattled Courage: The Experience of Combat in the American Civil War* (New York: Free Press, 1987), esp. 17–20; Michael C. C. Adams, *Fighting for Defeat: Union Military Failure in the East, 1861–1865* (originally published as *Our Masters the Rebels,* 1978) (Lincoln: University of Nebraska Press,

1992), esp. 27–28; C. Vann Woodward, ed., *Mary Chesnut's Civil War* (New Haven: Yale University Press, 1981), 376.

6. Horace Greeley, *The American Conflict: A History of the Great Rebellion . . . Intended to Exhibit Its Moral and Political Phases*, 2 vols. (Hartford, Ct.: O. D. Case, 1864), 1:499.

7. See, for example, Elbridge Gerry Spaulding, *A Resource of War . . . History of the Legal Tender Paper Money Issued during the Great Rebellion* (Buffalo, N.Y.: Express Printing, 1869). Wesley C. Mitchell, *A History of the Greenbacks, with Special Reference to the Economic Consequences of Their Issue, 1862–1865* (Chicago: University of Chicago Press, 1903), is a sober, academic, statistical study. Only financial histories of the period and an occasional polemic on labor are listed as published before 1910 in Allan Nevins, James I. Robertson, Jr., and Bell I. Wiley, eds., *Civil War Books: A Critical Bibliography*, 2 vols. (Baton Rouge: Louisiana State University Press, 1967–68), esp. 2:119–39.

8. Edwin A. Pratt, *The Rise of Rail-Power in War and Conquest, 1833–1914* (Philadelphia: J. B. Lippincott, 1916), 16, and for the extent of its use in track miles, 18. Pratt stated that the "extent to which railways are being used in this present War of the Nations has taken quite by surprise a world whose military historians, in their accounts of what armies have done or have failed to do on the battle-field in the past, have too often disregarded such matters of detail as to how the armies got there and the possible effect of good or defective transport conditions, including the maintenance of supplies and communications, on the whole course of a campaign" (vii). Pratt gave elaborate credit to the American Civil War for solving many of the problems of railroads in modern war, but he did not note any existing advantage to the North at the beginning of the war or in general relate the superior use of railways to northern economic civilization (see esp. ix).

9. Frederick Merk, *The Economic History of Wisconsin during the Civil War Decade* (1916; Madison: State Historical Society of Wisconsin, 1971), 7, 390.

10. Emerson D. Fite, *Social and Industrial Conditions in the North during the Civil War* (New York: Macmillan, 1910), v, 230–31, 151.

11. Clifford Dowdey, ed., *The Wartime Papers of R. E. Lee* (Boston: Little, Brown, 1961), 934.

12. See Pells, *Liberal Minds*, for some dissenters.

13. Paul Fussell, *Wartime: Understanding and Behavior in the Second World War* (New York: Oxford University Press, 1989), esp. 90–95.

14. Michael Sherry, *In the Shadow of War: The United States since the 1930s* (New Haven: Yale University Press, 1995), 162; Conyers Read, "The Social Responsibilities of the Historian," *American Historical Review* 55 (January 1950): 283. Sherry also suggests the image of a shadow for the effect of World War II on historiography.

15. Bernard DeVoto, "The Easy Chair," *Harper's* (February 1946): 123–26,

(March 1946): 234–37; Arthur M. Schlesinger, Jr., "The Causes of the Civil War: A Note on Historical Sentimentalism," *Partisan Review* (October 1949): 969–81; Thomas J. Pressly, *Americans Interpret Their Civil War* (New York: Free Press, 1954), 341–42. For the negative view of total war prevailing as World War II began, see esp. Fletcher Pratt, *America and Total War* (New York: Smith and Durrell, 1941). See also Ladislas Farago, ed., *The Axis Grand Strategy: Blueprints for a Total War* (New York: Farrar and Rinehart, 1942), esp. 3. For a decoupling of the idea of total war from its unfavorable associations with totalitarianism, see Kimball Young, "The Psychology of War," in *War as a Social Institution: The Historian's Perspective*, ed. Jesse D. Clarkson and Thomas C. Cochran (New York: Columbia University Press, 1941), esp. 10. More typical negative views prevailed in the same volume in B. Malinowski, "The Roots of War," esp. 22, 31, and H. A. De Weerd, "Civilian and Military Element in Modern War," esp. 111.

16. T. Harry Williams, "The Military Leadership of North and South," in *Why the North Won the Civil War*, ed. David Donald (Baton Rouge: Louisiana State University Press, 1960), 40, 44.

17. Norman A. Graebner, "Northern Diplomacy and European Neutrality," ibid., 58, 78; David Donald, "Died of Democracy," ibid., 79.

18. Mark E. Neely, Jr., "Was the Civil War a Total War?" *Civil War History* 37 (March 1991): 8–9; James M. McPherson, "Lincoln and the Second American Revolution," in *Abraham Lincoln and the American Political Tradition*, ed. John L. Thomas (Amherst: University of Massachusetts Press, 1986), 151. McPherson also used the "being terrible on the enemy" phrase in "Lincoln and the Strategy of Unconditional Surrender," in *Lincoln, the War President*, ed. Gabor S. Boritt (New York: Oxford University Press, 1992), 54. McPherson describes criticism of the "total war" theory as a "semantic" victory and defends the continued use of the idea as a Weberian "ideal type" in "From Limited to Total War, 1861–1865," in *Drawn with the Sword: Reflections on the American Civil War* (New York: Oxford University Press, 1996), esp. 67–70.

19. Charles Royster, *The Destructive War: William Tecumseh Sherman, Stonewall Jackson, and the Americans* (New York: Knopf, 1991), 241.

20. Neely, "Was the Civil War a Total War?" 8; Eric Foner, *Reconstruction: America's Unfinished Revolution, 1863–1877* (New York: Harper and Row, 1988), 7, 18.

21. Michael Eliot Howard, *Clausewitz* (New York: Oxford University Press, 1983), 49; Peter Paret, *Understanding War: Essays on Clausewitz and Military Power* (Princeton: Princeton University Press, 1992), 109. They call the idea escalation.

22. Roy P. Basler, Marion Dolores Pratt, and Lloyd A. Dunlap, eds., *Collected Works of Abraham Lincoln*, 9 vols. (New Brunswick, N.J.: Rutgers University Press, 1953–55), 6:408.

23. Ibid., 7:330–31; Michael Fellman, *Citizen Sherman: A Life of William Tecumseh Sherman* (New York: Random House, 1995), 177.

24. Basler, Pratt, and Dunlap, eds., *Collected Works*, 7:493.

25. *The War of the Rebellion: A Compilation of the Official Records of the Union and Confederate Armies* (Washington, D.C.: U.S. Government Printing Office, 1880–1901), ser. 1, vol. 37, pt. 2, p. 366.

26. Ibid., ser. 1, vol. 37, pt. 2, p. 592 (Early's orders), p. 515 (Averell to Couch); Gideon Welles, *Diary of Gideon Welles, Secretary of the Navy under Lincoln and Johnson* (Boston: Houghton Mifflin, 1911), 3:87, 96. At the time, Hunter's depredations were a touchy issue, but they have since lost significance. The ever-protective Horace Porter was careful to say, "The stringent orders given by Grant to Sigel, and by him turned over to Hunter, who had succeeded him, were prepared with a view to preventing all wanton destruction." Porter noted, however, "Notwithstanding these orders, there were some houses burned and damage done to individual property during this raid" (Porter, *Campaigning with Grant* [1897; New York: DaCapo, 1986], 236).

27. Mark Grimsley, *The Hard Hand of War: Union Military Policy toward Southern Civilians* (Cambridge: Cambridge University Press, 1995); Eric T. Dean, Jr., "Rethinking the Civil War: Beyond 'Revolutions,' 'Reconstructions,' and the 'New Social History,'" *Southern Historian* 15 (1994): 28–50. The idea is far from dead, however: see Lance Janda, "Shutting the Gates of Mercy: The American Origins of Total War, 1860–1880," *Journal of Military History* 59 (January 1995): 7–26; and Daniel E. Sutherland, "Abraham Lincoln, John Pope, and the Origins of Total War," *Journal of Military History* 56 (October 1992): 567–86, esp. 568n.

28. Janda, "Shutting the Gates," 8, 11, 22.

29. Robert M. Utley, *Frontiersmen in Blue: The United States Army and the Indian, 1848–1865* (New York: Macmillan, 1967), 346–47.

30. Robert M. Utley, *Frontier Regulars: The United States Army and the Indian, 1866–1891* (New York: Macmillan, 1973), 51–52, 144.

31. Perry D. Jamieson, *Crossing the Deadly Ground: United States Army Tactics, 1865–1899* (Tuscaloosa: University of Alabama Press, 1994), 36–53. Jamieson acknowledges Robert Wooster's modest dissent in *The Military and the United States Indian Policy, 1865–1903* (New Haven: Yale University Press, 1988), 135–44. Wooster concluded that Sherman and Sheridan "eventually" embraced total war against Indians, while most of their fellow officers did not. A more recent article, Janda, "Shutting the Gates," finds that "the tactics of the Indian wars bear a remarkable similarity to methods employed during the Civil War" (25).

32. Michael Fellman, *Inside War: The Guerrilla Conflict in Missouri during the American Civil War* (New York: Oxford University Press, 1988), esp. 213–14.

33. Mark E. Neely, Jr., *The Abraham Lincoln Encyclopedia* (New York: McGraw-Hill, 1982), 160–61.

34. David Herbert Donald, *Lincoln* (New York: Simon and Schuster, 1995), 207.

35. Edmund Wilson, *Patriotic Gore: Studies in the Literature of the American Civil War* (New York: Oxford University Press, 1961), 115, 118.

Robert E. Lee, posing for a famous portrait by Mathew Brady. Courtesy Library of Congress.

Considering *Lee Considered:*
Robert E. Lee and the Lost Cause

Alan T. Nolan

THE NATIONALLY DISTRIBUTED *Civil War News* of October 1992 printed a reader's letter that said, in part, "I call upon every true student of the Civil War, every son and daughter of the veterans of that war, North and South, and every organization formed to study, research, reenact, preserve and remember our Civil War heritage not to purchase Nolan's book. ... If you have already, burn it. ... Moreover, it is noted that Nolan's name has appeared on the agenda as a presenter at certain Civil War symposiums. ... I recommend that you not attend and write to the sponsor stating why."[1] The letter was signed by a retired general of the U.S. Army who also sent copies to a broad segment of Civil War media and organizations. The book in question was my 1991 work, *Lee Considered: General Robert E. Lee and Civil War History.*

I was intimidated to find myself included in the group of distinguished professional historians who spoke at this conference. I cite the letter as a credential, because I doubt if any of the other participants has caused such a letter to be written.

As further background, I confess that I am interested in myths and legends, especially ones that defy facts or, even more curious, coexist with facts while contradicting them. The Irish writer Sean

O'Faolain tells of a woman of his acquaintance in West Cork. As is well known, the Irish have a large and colorful mythology that includes a number of mythical creatures—fairies, elves, leprechauns, and other "Wee Folk." O'Faolain asked his friend if she really believed in the Wee Folk. She responded, "Of course not, but they are there!" It is my opinion that what is deemed to be the history of the Civil War is heavily marked by this phenomenon.

I believe that in the popular mind the Civil War exists as an American counterpart of an Icelandic saga. According to the dictionary, a *saga* is a "story of heroic deeds." Perhaps *legend* would be a more descriptive term, defined as "any story coming down from the past, especially one popularly taken as historical though not verifiable; also such stories and traditions collectively, especially of a particular people." That legends commonly persist is a fact to which I may be more sensitive than my colleagues because round tables and Civil War seminars are more my milieu than is a gathering of professional historians. I insist that the legend exists and that it is more popularly entrenched than the history of the period. Indeed, it serves as the history of the period.

Gaines M. Foster wrote of the way in which the war generation of southerners and succeeding generations "accepted defeat and interpreted the war in the years from 1865 to 1913. . . . Their interpretation emerged in what has come to be called the Lost Cause, the postwar writings and activities that perpetuated the memory of the Confederacy." Having identified the southern memorial organizations, Foster contends that "more Southerners formed an understanding of their past through the ceremonial activities or rituals conducted by these groups than through anything else."[2] The Lost Cause, as I will call it today, is the legend of the Civil War.

The legend, as distinguished from the history of the war, has certain characteristics. Thus, the conflict is presented as essentially romantic, a contest of honor and martial glory in which brave and valorous men and women contended over the issue of Southern independence. The romantic image of the war contrasts sharply with reality. The war was in fact harsh and cruel, producing not only astonishing fatalities—in excess of 600,000 men—but also thousands of disabled soldiers, widows, and orphans. These casualties and guerrilla warfare, border-state struggles, prison camps, and widespread destruction of southern cities justify Robert Penn Warren's characterization of the war:

> The word *tragedy* is often used loosely. Here we use it at its deepest significance: the image in action of the deepest questions of man's fate and man's attitude toward his fate. For the Civil War is, massively, that. It is the story of a crime of monstrous inhumanity, into which almost innocently men stumbled; of consequences which could not be trammeled up, and of men who tangled themselves more and more vindictively and desperately until the powers of reason were twisted and their virtues perverted.[3]

The legend is also marked by defensive Confederate advocacy. As pointed out by Michael C. C. Adams in *Our Masters the Rebels*, long before the secession crisis, southerners "came to see themselves as representing a minority group within the nation," in part because of "the need to justify the existence of slavery. . . . Even before the abolitionist attacks from the North, Southerners began the defense of slavery as a social system that provided unique benefits, both for the slave whom it placed under the fatherly care of a superior race and for the master who was given the freedom from toil necessary to the creation of a superior culture."[4] In short, the southerners were placed in a defensive posture before the war, and this status has never changed. This defensive apologetic stance has been carried over into what is deemed the history of the war, what I am calling the Lost Cause legend.

Elements of the Lost Cause Legend

SLAVERY AND THE WAR

It has always seemed clear to me that the slavery issue was the common denominator of the national political discord in the generation before the war. And surely it is not a coincidence that the compromise efforts between the time of South Carolina's secession and the firing on Fort Sumter were concerned with the status of slavery. Despite these facts, some historians argued until recently that slavery was not the central issue between the sections; it was trivialized as the cause of the war in favor of such things as tariff disputes, control of investment banking, cultural differences, and conflict between industrial and agricultural societies. Today's historians seem to concede that the South seceded to protect slavery and that the North went to war to defeat secession. Slavery therefore caused the war. I believe, however, that in the popular mind slavery remains discounted as the cause of the war. We know, for example, that there was an outcry about Ken Burns's PBS Civil War series because it so categorically identified slavery as the cause of the war.

The Abolitionists

The status of the abolitionists in the legend is a corollary to the principle that slavery was not the cause of the war. The abolitionists' image is negative. They were troublemakers, provocateurs, virtually manufacturing a disagreement that was of little or no substance. Reformers are always painful people, simply because they will not cooperate, and they demand the reluctant attention of those who will. Reformers frequently provoke unpleasant feelings of guilt in others. But the abolitionists were right one hundred years ago. It is now late in the twentieth century. There is no excuse for their negative image in a historical sense, but the image persists in the legend.

The South Would Have Given It Up

A third principle of the Lost Cause teaches that slavery would have been abandoned by the South on its own. It was simply a question of time. If the war *was* about slavery, fighting was unnecessary for the elimination of the institution. This contention conveniently overlooks the agitation over the acquisition of Cuba and the filibustering about Mexican and South American territory. I believe that Allan Nevins was correct when he said, "The South, as a whole, in 1846–61, was not moving toward emancipation, but away from it. It was not relaxing the laws which guarded the system, but reinforcing them. It was not ameliorating slavery, but making it harsher and more implacable. The South was further from a just solution of the slavery problem in 1830 than it had been in 1789. It was further from a tenable solution in 1860 than it had been in 1830."[5]

THE SLAVES

Related to the principles that I have mentioned are the "faithful slave" myth and what William Garrett Piston calls the "happy darky stereotype."[6] Fiction writers from Joel Chandler Harris to Margaret Mitchell and their counterparts in an earlier Hollywood are largely responsible for these historical problems. Recall Shirley Temple playing the part of a southern plantation daughter, tap dancing in the big house with Bill "Bojangles" Robinson, who was a happy slave. *The Little Colonel* (1935) was a typical Hollywood view of slavery. Presumably, there were slaves who were fond of and sympathetic toward their owners, fitting the unknowing and uncaring "happy darky" mold. But this image was for so long the predominant portrayal that it became endemic to the popular legend. Only recently laypeople learned of the significant Federal logistical problems caused by the slaves' fleeing to the Federal lines and of the slaves' assisting Federal soldiers in the field. Despite the work of James McPherson and Dudley Cornish, the facts concerning black soldiers in the Federal army are new information to many Americans. It seems especially unfortunate to me that African Americans have not known of this heritage. When I saw the movie *Glory,* a number of blacks were in the audience. I overheard them expressing surprise that "we were in the Civil War." The actor Denzel Washington had a strong role in the film. A sophisticated and well-educated black man, he has reported his own amazement when the script was initially sent to him because he was unaware that black soldiers had served in the Union army.

The Nationalistic/Cultural Difference

Having eliminated slavery as the source of sectional contention, the South created a nationalistic/cultural basis for the disagreement. This theory was instituted on the eve of the war and became a staple of the Lost Cause theory after the war. An extensive statement of the argument appeared in June 1860 in the *Southern Literary Messenger*. The northerners were said to be descended from the Anglo-Saxon tribes that had been conquered by the Norman cavaliers. The Norman cavaliers were, of course, the ancestors of the southerners, according to this theory. It was written that the cavaliers were "descended from the Norman Barons of William the Conqueror, a race distinguished in its earliest history for its warlike and fearless character, a race in all times since renowned for its gallantry, chivalry, honor, gentleness, and intellect."[7] As described in *Why the South Lost the Civil War*, the South "simply appropriated as their own the history they shared with the Union and recreated it. . . . Without its own distinctive past upon which to base its nationality, the Confederacy appropriated history and created a mythic past of exiled cavaliers and chivalrous knights that owed more to Sir Walter Scott than to the flesh and blood migrants from the Old World."[8] Kenneth Stampp has commented on this fiction, "Fundamentally [the Confederacy] was not the product of genuine Southern nationalism; indeed, except for the institution of slavery, the South had little to give it a clear national identity . . . and the notion of a distinct Southern culture was largely a figment of the romantic imaginations of a handful of intellectuals and proslavery propagandists."[9] Grady McWhiney, David M. Potter, and other current historians share Stampp's opinion.

Military Analysis

The legend has also rationalized the Confederate loss in the war's military aspects. It was asserted, in effect, that the South could not have won the war because of its manpower and material disadvantages.[10] On the other hand—never mind the contradiction—it was stated that if the Confederacy had won at Gettysburg, it would have won the war. The Gettysburg loss was attributed to General James Longstreet. By extension, Longstreet was responsible for the loss of the war. Foster calls this the "Longstreet lost it at Gettysburg" theory. It became part of the legend.[11]

Understanding the Reason for the Legend

Warren wrote that "the Civil War is our only 'felt' history—history lived in the national imagination."[12] I believe that imagination is the stuff of legend. Bruce Catton has expressed the same idea in a different way: "For above and beyond everything else, the Civil War was a matter of emotions. It came about because men's emotions ran away with them; it was borne, North and South, for four mortal years because these emotions remained strong; and its first significance, nowadays, is often more a matter for the heart than for the head."[13] These insights set up a psychological source for the legend. The imaginative and predominantly emotional sense of the Civil War arose because it was marked by such intense contradictions and traumas.

The primary contradiction was that between the Declaration of Independence and the existence and flourishing of slavery. It is important to acknowledge that both sections were mired in this conflict. Although a majority of the northern people believed by 1860 that slavery should not be extended, the same majority accepted slavery where it existed and would not and did not go to war to extinguish slavery. Secession to protect slavery precipitated the war, and slavery became a victim of the war for a combination of military and political reasons.

With further regard to contradictions, predominant northern attitudes about race were not, of themselves, significantly different from those in the South. The free black population was severely discriminated against in civil and social rights. In several states, notably those of the Midwest, state constitutions prohibited the immigration of free blacks. Abraham Lincoln said in 1858 that he opposed "the social and political equality"[14] of the races, surely the predominant attitude of the northern people. Thus, the antislavery movement in the North struggled with an interior conflict—a conviction that slavery was wrong side by side with a crude and virulent racism.

Southern supporters of slavery also had contradictory feelings. On the one hand, southern leaders and theologians proclaimed that slavery was a positive good for master and slave alike. On the other hand, the southern leadership class was religiously orthodox. The southerners sensed a discrepancy between their historic faith and the new faith in slavery. In addition, lascivious connections between masters and female slaves lingered in the system. In a society that boasted of chivalry, morality, and racial purity, the sexual side of slavery was a disturbing, dirty, and open secret. Further, the whole Western world was arrayed against the southern view, as many of the Founding Fathers had been, and they were much respected and imitated by the planter aristocracy. The mixture of religious tradition, the standards of Western culture, and the theories of the supporters of the institution created what Bell I. Wiley identifies as a widespread "sense of guilt" in the Southern leadership.[15] Calling this "crypto-emancipationism," Warren describes it as "a deep moral, logical, and economic unease" about slavery.[16] That this ambiguity existed in the South is suggested by the Confederate constitution. While expressly protecting the ownership of slaves, it forbade the slave trade, an implicit acknowledgment that something was wrong about slavery.

But there is more to the story of contradictions. The South had an ancient loyalty to the United States and a culture that it shared with the North, at least in broad terms. Again to quote Warren, "the nation share[d] deep and significant convictions and [was] not a mere hand basket of factions huddled arbitrarily together by historical happen-so."[17] The sections shared the same revolutionary experience, heroes, and Founding Fathers. The South departed from the Bill of Rights in its efforts to protect slavery but at bottom shared a sense of political values with the North. It is worthwhile again to refer to Stampp:

> Fundamentally [the Confederacy] was not the product of genuine Southern nationalism; indeed, except for the institution of slavery, the South had little to give it a clear national identity. It had no natural frontiers; its white population came from the same stocks as the Northern population; its political tradition and religious beliefs were not significantly different from those of the North; it had no history of its own; and the notion of a distinct Southern culture was largely a figment of the romantic imaginations of a handful of intellectuals and pro-slavery propagandists.
>
> Even after a generation of intense sectional conflict over slavery, the South was still bound to the Union by heritage of national ideals and traditions.[18]

This southern inability to separate itself emotionally from the common ground it shared with the North had a predictable result. As the authors of *Why the South Lost the Civil War* point out, "A truly nationalistic movement will not be confused about where its loyalties lie. Yet this was a great source of Confederate confusion. . . . Southerners did indeed suffer a confusion of loyalties."[19] This confusion provided another significant contradiction to add to the list.

Common nationalism and culture drew the participants into another contradiction. Although fighting with incredible ferocity, enlisted men and officers tended to trust one another and had difficulty identifying each other as genuine enemies. The books are full of stories of meetings and friendly personal contacts between picket lines. Many general officers had been at West Point together or had been stationed together at isolated prewar military posts and regarded themselves as friends. Grant's *Memoirs* and Porter Alexander's *Fighting for the Confederacy* describe the immediate postsurrender fraternization of officers and men of both armies at Appomattox.

Finally, regarding trauma as a source of the legend was the awfulness of the event. I have already quoted Warren about the scope and depth of the tragedy, "a crime of monstrous inhumanity." The recent and relatively sophisticated advances in ordnance and the contrasting primitiveness of the sciences of medicine, nutrition, and sanitation combined to create unusual deprivation and suffering. In short, the Civil War as a human event was so rife with contradictions and

traumas, and so confused and painful in its images, that the participants were moved to manufacture a history of the event. They were
psychologically impelled to obscure the truth with tales and traditions that were essentially romantic and more palatable than the facts.
This phenomenon constitutes one of the sources of the legend.

Another source of the legend lay in the participants' need to rationalize the war in social terms. Somehow they had to account for
themselves. While proclaiming the righteousness of the cause, the
South had to accept a bitter and destructive defeat. James M.
McPherson has accurately summed up the war's consequences for
the South: "The South was not only invaded and conquered, it was
utterly destroyed. By 1865 the Union forces had . . . destroyed two-
thirds of the assessed value of southern wealth, two-fifths of the
South's livestock, and one-quarter of her white men between the ages
of twenty and forty. More than half of the farm machinery was ru-
ined, and the damage to railroads and industry was incalculable."[20]
The South needed to justify itself.

The North had more complicated rationalizing to do. On the
one hand, it needed to establish that it had been right, that the war
had been worth the cost. But insisting that the two sections comprised one nation, the North needed to reclaim the allegiance of the
South, creating an implicit northern disposition to protect the dignity of the South to bind it again to the Union. The North surely
perceived that this apology would be difficult because of the southern wounds.

There was, to be sure, an initial period of bitterness and a pro-
tracted period of maneuvering as the national political parties
sought to establish their southern constituencies. In the North,
"bloody shirt" politics was practiced in the interest of Republican
political control. Prior to the Hayes-Tilden compromise of 1877,
there were Federal efforts to guarantee and protect the rights of
the freedmen. But in the longer run, the South's need to dignify its
defeat and losses and the northern need to credit the Southern cause
in the interest of political union prevailed. Just as the psychological motive produced a romantic mask for the war's inhumanity, the

participants' need to justify themselves dictated the alteration of critical facts concerning the war.

Because the long-standing disagreement, and the war itself, had been about slavery and the status of the black race, it is not surprising that the social rationalizations about the war started with these matters. Two significant themes were developed in the South. The first concerned the role of slavery. The second involved changing the sense of the slave and the freedman.

Stampp commented that southerners "denied that slavery had anything to do with the Confederate cause, thus decontaminating it and turning it into something they could cherish. After Appomattox, Jefferson Davis claimed that slavery 'was in no wise the cause of the conflict,' and Alexander H. Stephens argued that the war 'was not a contest between the advocates or opponents of that peculiar institution.'"[21] According to Robert F. Durden, this denial became "a cardinal element of the Southern apologia."[22] Indeed, James L. Roark found that southerners had "a nearly universal desire to escape the ignominy attached to slavery."[23]

The new picture of the southern black also required a stark reversal. In place of the slaves and freedmen that existed in fact, there emerged, as previously noted, the "happy darky stereotype." This person—unaware, unknowing, and uncaring—became universally known, North as well as South.

By eliminating slavery as the issue that had divided the North and South and led them into the war, and by changing the image of the real black person to that of the happy darky, the southern leadership facilitated northern acceptance of the honor of the South. It is, of course, not surprising that the South discarded the protection of slavery as the reason for its conduct. States' rights, liberty, and the Constitution were surely more likely rationales for secession. It also is not surprising that the South was anxious to create the happy darky, who replaced a much more complex and threatening person, the real slave and freedman.

The revisionism in regard to slavery as a cause of the war and the nature of the slaves could have remained a southern theme. It could not have become part of the national legend without northern complicity, and the North, including its historians, did accept the South's rewriting of the record. It let the South substitute a war for liberty for the war for slavery, and the North ceased to think of the slaves and freedmen as serious persons. This northern contribution to the legend resulted in part from its implicit need to credit the South. In this process, it was necessary for slavery protection to be disregarded as the reason for secession because the truth about slavery's relationship to the war interjected a divisive element, a moral disagreement, into the reunification efforts of whites, North and South. The essential thrust of the reunification effort was that "both sides were right." If the war had concerned freedom, both sides could not have been right. Therefore, the involvement of freedom had to go.

And the North was willing to participate in the revising of history simply because of racism itself. In spite of the differences between northern and southern views of slavery, the two sections shared an intense antagonism toward black people. The northern fear and dislike helped persuade the North that it surely would not have caused such a fuss about an insignificant thing like the circumstances of these black people. The South was right, after all; slavery had not been the source of conflict between the sections.

Racism therefore gave the North a reason to accept the South's rationalization of the cause of the war and the change in the image of the freedman. Racism was also perceived as a social value in itself. It was a common ground between the sections and was therefore a unifying force. Slavery was discounted as the source of difficulty between the sections; then, identified as essentially ignorant and comic bystanders or helpmates to their owners, blacks were dropped from the history of the war. That they had fled into the Federal lines, had performed invaluable service to Federal soldiers, had joined the Federal army in large numbers—as many as 180,000[24]—and had fought and died for the United States were simply dropped from history. This revisionism met the social needs of both sections and served the North's racist antagonism. It also helped to seal reunion and affirm southern honor.

Because it struck at the basic truths of the war, the false treatment of slavery and black people had a significant effect on the establishment of the Civil War as legend. Removed from their real role as the issue, their actual participation in the fighting ignored, the blacks were characterized as historically irrelevant. Racism became a motivation and prominent characteristic of the legendary treatment of the war.

The disregard of slavery and of the authentic black people carried a steep price in terms of historical meaning. The war was deprived of any high purpose or significance. The North was pictured as having for no significant reason acted in such a way within the prewar political process as to provoke secession. A void was substituted for antislavery sentiment as the source of disagreement between the sections. The revised account also meant that the North had then bloodily defeated secession simply for the purpose of forcing the southerners to remain a part of the nation against their own will.

The disregard of slavery unhinged cause and effect in regard to the war. The void of cause and effect did not remain. The historians promptly came forward. An endless string of hypotheses about the origins of the war was put together. Thomas J. Pressly's *Americans Interpret Their Civil War* remains a comprehensive statement of account of this historiography.[25] Gaines Foster pointed out that in this accounting, southern culture was frequently portrayed as superior, something "blessed," a world peopled by "cavalier aristocrats or martyrs" as well as by the happy darky. "Grace and gentility," according to Foster, were attributed to the prewar South, and Piston noted that there also "developed a romanticized stereotype of the Confederate soldier."[26] These changes in the facts supplemented and reinforced the melodrama that had been created to mask the terrible tragedy of the war. Margaret Mitchell's *Gone with the Wind* is an orthodox statement of the legend, the twentieth century's most well-known Civil War story. It idealizes the men and women of the planter class, pictures southern manhood as having superior courage, finds gentility in the planter aristocracy in spite of slavery, exaggerates the material disadvantages of the South's armies, and portrays the Yankees as bushwhackers. The slaves are pictured as the simple, happy, and devoted companions of their owners. As indicated earlier, the legend also rationalized the Southern defeat in a military sense.

The sections' social justifications had profound consequences. Reunion was facilitated and southern honor assured, but truth was lost in the process, as were equal protection of the laws, a promise of the Fourteenth Amendment, and the Fifteenth Amendment's guarantee of suffrage for blacks.

The legend of the war, still prevailing, resulted from a combination of the war's actual contradictions and traumas and the postwar social rationalizations of the participants. Both elements contributed to the fictions that made the legend. They produced romance in place of realism and significant distortions of critical facts. The legend seems to exist "in our bones" and defeats the efforts of today's historians to set it straight.

The Warrior Hero

The legend of the Civil War persists. It is a tale of glory. Because the truth of the cause of the war—the slavery disagreement—has been muted, it is a story of military competition between brave people for no particular reason other than the honor of it all.

An invariable character of the literary form called the legend is the Warrior Hero, the great man of superior personality and skill, a superman, a savior. General Lee supplies this role in the Civil War legend. He is the personification of the American romance of the Civil War. I was drawn to wonder about the legend itself and about how and why it existed and about Lee as a character in the legend. Thomas L. Connelly and others have studied the construction of the Lee tradition. I decided to inquire into its merits—that is, to try to determine the extent to which the Lee tradition is historical.

Although Douglas Southall Freeman wrote the landmark book about Lee as the Warrior Hero, he was not the first romancer. Writing in 1868, Fanny Downing described Lee as "bathed in the white light which falls directly upon him from the smile of an approving and sustaining God."[27] By 1880 this process had advanced considerably. John W. Daniel of General Jubal A. Early's staff wrote, "The Divinity in [Lee's] bosom shown translucent through the man, and his spirit rose up the Godlike."[28] As especially related to the O'Faolain phenomenon, Sir Frederick Maurice called Lee a "stout Democrat,"[29] in spite of Lee's scorn of the "immigrants from abroad" and people "from the slums of the city" who had fought for the North.[30] Writing in 1912, Gamaliel Bradford asserted that "in fighting for the Confederacy, Lee was fighting for slavery, and he must have known perfectly well that if the South triumphed and maintained its independence, slavery would grow and flourish for another generation, if not for a century. . . . This man, fighting as he believed, for freedom, for independence, for democracy, was fighting also to rivet the shackles more firmly on millions of his fellow men." But on the very next page, Bradford also rhapsodized about Lee: "In Lee, no pride, but virtue all; not liberty for himself alone, but for others, for everyone."[31] The man who fought for an additional generation or perhaps one hundred years more of slavery was magically transformed into a man who wanted liberty for everyone.

And then of course there is Freeman. In addition to anonymous and unverifiable anecdotes about Lee the man, Freeman rationalized every blemish, always blamed Lee's subordinates for military failures, and emasculated documents that would mar this characterization. The most dramatic example of this documentary phenomenon is his selective quotation from Lee's January 11, 1865, letter about putting slaves into the Confederate army. To support his claim that Lee was an emancipationist, Freeman quotes that portion of the letter in which the general suggested emancipation to induce the slaves to fight for the Confederacy. But he omits Lee's statement in the same letter that slavery was "the best" relationship between the races and his comment on the "evil consequences to both races" from emancipation.[32] In the final analysis, Freeman was quite candid about the subject of his writing. In *The South to Posterity*, Freeman set forth a critical bibliography of books about the war. He acknowledged that he was "interested to ascertain which were the books that seemed to have made new protagonists for the South." He sought to identify the books "that have brought a new generation of Americans to an understanding of the Southern point of view."[33] Freeman, whose biography of Lee is a standard reference book, clearly was writing as an advocate.

Lee Considered had a specific, limited purpose, to examine historically six particular characteristics attributed to Lee as the Warrior Hero: his antislavery views, the manner and circumstances of his decision to secede, his generalship, his alleged magnanimity toward the North, his continued fighting after he believed that defeat was inevitable, and his alleged role as a postwar conciliator.

With regard to the peculiar institution, American culture clearly would want a hero of its legend to have been antislavery, as has been widely proclaimed about Lee. In an 1856 letter he wrote that slavery was "a moral & political evil," but he also wrote that slavery was "necessary" for the slaves' "instruction as a race." Further, he trafficked in slaves, saw to the recapture of fugitive slaves from Arlington, identified the maintenance of slavery as a Confederate war aim, and, of course, fought vigorously for the Confederacy. Late in the war, as noted earlier, he wrote that slavery was "the best" relationship that can exist between the races. I concluded that Lee was not antislavery in any meaningful, practical sense.

Although he disapproved of secession, Lee decided early in the crisis that he would go south under certain circumstances and surely would follow Virginia. While he was in this conditional state of mind, on March 15, 1861, the Confederate government offered him a brigadier generalship, the highest commission authorized by the Confederacy, and he neither accepted nor rejected it. Then on March 30, 1861, he accepted a Federal commission as colonel. The Virginia Convention voted to secede on April 17, and one day later, Lee rejected a Federal command. On April 20, 1861, he posted his resignation from the U.S. Army, and, without waiting for its acceptance pursuant to army regulations, agreed at once to go to Richmond to see the Virginia governor. On April 22 he accepted a major generalship from Virginia and command of its forces. His correspondence at the time suggested to others that he sought a passive role in the conflict and did not acknowledge the competition for his services in high command. He also did not suggest that he would accept such a significant role in the Confederacy. Thus, well aware of the competition for his services in high command, on the day of his resignation and two days before accepting the Virginia commission, he wrote to his sister that it was his "sincere hope that my poor services may never be needed." On the same day, he wrote to his brother telling of his resignation and classified himself as "a private citizen" with "no other ambition than to remain at home."[34] I concluded that Lee's ambiguity suggested a lack of candor and too fine a line between loyalty to the United States and to the Confederacy.

To Jefferson Davis, Lee stated his strategic grasp of the war: "If we can defeat or drive the armies of the enemy from the field, we shall have peace. All our efforts and energies should be devoted to that object." Thus, Lee relied on the unrealistic goal of military defeat of the North instead of seeking to win by not losing. Accordingly, in the words of J. F. C. Fuller, Lee "rushed forth to find a battlefield, to challenge a contest between himself and the North."[35]

Regarding his military leadership, especially during 1862 and 1863, Lee was much too aggressive and consequently suffered unnecessary, irreplaceable, and disproportionate casualties. He surely accomplished marked tactical successes, but the price of these victories, which could have been avoided by a more defensive strategy, progressively deprived his army of maneuverability and led it into a fatal siege. His admirers insist on remarking on his successes, one battle at a time, and do not evaluate the consequences of his aggressive approach to the war. One admiring biographer unwittingly made this point, noting that Lee went "from one victory that led nowhere to another" and referring to Lee's "glorious . . . campaign filled with victories that resulted in total defeat."[36]

The nationalistic legend needed a hero who was not bitter about the North. Accordingly, the legend insists that Lee felt only charitably toward the northerners. But the open and notorious written record shows him referring to the Federals as "vandals," people who would carry off southern women, people full of "malice & revenge." He wrote that they would persecute his wife and rejoice at the death of a Confederate soldier's wife; they were "cowardly persecutors," "unchristian & atrocious."[37]

It is apparent that Lee believed that the cause was lost perhaps as early as Gettysburg and Vicksburg and at the latest when Lincoln was reelected. Was fighting on in these circumstances necessarily heroic? In General Order no. 9, issued on April 10, 1865, Lee said that he had surrendered at Appomattox "to avoid the useless sacrifice" of his soldiers. In advising Davis of the surrender, after the fact, he relied on avoiding further deaths and stated, "I did not see how a surrender could have been avoided."[38] I pose two questions on this point: (1) Did Lee do the right thing on April 9, 1865, when he surrendered his army for the reasons he reported at the time? (2) If the answer to that question is in the affirmative, at what earlier time would his surrender have been appropriate?

After the war Lee was on occasion conciliatory, but he was much more of a bitter sectional advocate with deep antagonism toward the northerners and toward the freedmen. In May 1865 while visiting with his cousin, Thomas H. Carter, Lee advised Carter not to depend for labor on the ninety or so blacks who still lived on the Carter farm. According to Lee, the government would provide for the blacks, and Carter should employ white people.[39] On March 12, 1868, in a letter to his son, Robert, who had taken up farming, Lee advised, "You will never prosper with blacks, and it is abhorrent to a reflecting mind to be supporting and cherishing those who are plotting and working for your injury, and all of whose sympathies and associations are antagonistic to yours. . . . Our material, social and political interests are naturally with the whites."[40] In terms of his attitude toward the North, in 1868 he wrote a letter regarding the impeachment of President Andrew Johnson in which he said, "I grieve for posterity, for American principles and American liberty. Our boasted self Govt. is fast becoming the jeer and laughing-stock of the world."[41] And in 1870, the year of his death, he told his colleague William

Preston Johnston of the "vindictiveness and malignity of the Yankees, of which he had no conception before the war."[42]

Conclusion

People who write seek an engagement with readers. Typically, except for friends and family, the readers whose reactions the writer is aware of are the reviewers. *Lee Considered* received its fair share of reviews, and the reviewers' reactions were remarkably diverse.

There were favorable reviews from reviewers who recognized the point of the book, most notably Drew Gilpin Faust and William S. McFeely.[43] There were also reviewers who did not like the book. Some simply denounced the book on its face. They, by God, just didn't like it. Others at least informed me of their concerns. The book asserted that the South had seceded to protect slavery and that slavery was therefore the cause of the war. Several contended that this was either an oversimplification or was not so. Some dissenters objected to the criticism of Lee as a military leader, citing his tactical brilliance at such places as Chancellorsville. The chapter concerning Lee's prolonging of the war was objectionable to some who pointed out that according to nineteenth-century mores there was no alternative to Lee's actions.

I did discover ruefully how disabling being a lawyer is. Almost invariably negative reviewers emphasized that I am a lawyer. Several referred to the book as a "lawyer's brief." To a lawyer, a brief is an argument based on the facts. This is not what the reviewers were suggesting.

Piston has remarked on the difficulty of overturning cultural roles in history. I recognize this problem, but I think that history would be served if the romance, the glorification, was removed from what is presented as Civil War history. I would like for the legend to give way to the harsh facts of the matter: the war was all about slavery, resulted from a failure of American politics, and was, as Warren says, "a crime of monstrous inhumanity." It did not resolve the American racial conflict. The South and the North simply adopted a different form of alienation of black people.

In terms of Lee's personal characteristics, Lee writers tend to outdo each other in describing his virtues and heroism, frequently by using hyperbole and comparisons of Lee to sublime standards or well-identified, sublime personages. A random sample of these techniques is informative. I noted Downing's and Daniel's descriptions of Lee. Maurice assured us that Lee was "a stout democrat." Marshall Fishwick described Lee as "Apollo on horseback," "the general on the beautiful white horse, fighting bravely as did the knights of old." Fishwick also saw Lee as "St. George slaying Yankee dragons" *and* St. Francis of Assisi because "literally everything and everybody loved him."[44] Charles Bracelen Flood wrote that Lee was a "confederate Santa Claus."[45] Freeman sprinkled his narrative with winsome anecdotes: Lee rescued a baby bird under enemy fire; Lee succored a wounded Federal soldier; Lee carried a child from a burning building; Lee played with children during the war; Lee stopped to pray with his soldiers in the face of Federal artillery fire. On the last page of his four-volume biography, Freeman pictured Lee as an imitation of Christ in a scene in which a young mother brought her baby for him to bless. Clifford Dowdey also frequently described Lee in christological terms, the war as passion play with Lee as Christ.

The problem is that the elaborate praising of Lee pertains not only to the general himself. It also extends to the context of his life and the causes, conduct, and consequences of the Civil War. It defines the character of Lee's contemporaries and his Federal adversaries. Adulation of Lee may not be history, but it could be harmless. It is not harmless because in the apotheosis process the issues of the war and other people of the war are misrepresented or diminished. The trivialization of slavery as the reason for secession and the establishment of the Confederacy is an example. It is in part a consequence of the creation of the stainless Lee who could not appear in the legend as leading slavery's army. The diminution of Grant and, to an even greater extent, of Lee's lieutenants—Longstreet, Richard B. Ewell of Gettysburg, and J. E. B. Stuart of Gettysburg—are examples. Justifying Lee required the diminution of these generals. Thus, history would be served if the stained-glass writing about Lee was eliminated.

As long as the legend persists, Lee's role will not change. He will remain the Warrior Hero of the legend. But if history replaces the legend, Lee will become a historical character of human proportions, and Civil War history will be more accurate.

Notes

1. *Civil War News,* October 1992.

2. Gaines M. Foster, *Ghosts of the Confederacy* (New York: Oxford University Press, 1987), 4.

3. Robert Penn Warren, *The Legacy of the Civil War* (New York: Random House, 1961), 102.

4. Michael C. C. Adams, *Our Masters the Rebels* (Cambridge: Harvard University Press, 1978), 3–4.

5. Allan Nevins, *The Emergence of Lincoln,* 2 vols. (New York: Charles Scribner's Sons, 1950), 2:468.

6. William Garrett Piston, *Lee's Tarnished Lieutenant: James Longstreet and His Place in Southern History* (Athens: University of Georgia Press, 1987), 157–58.

7. *Southern Literary Messenger* 30 (June 1860): 401–9.

8. Richard E. Beringer, Herman Hattaway, Archer Jones, and William N. Still, Jr., *Why the South Lost the Civil War* (Athens: University of Georgia Press, 1986), 76.

9. Kenneth M. Stampp, *The Imperiled Union* (New York: Oxford University Press, 1980), 255–56.

10. Foster, *Ghosts,* 57.

11. Ibid., 58.

12. Warren, *Legacy,* 4.

13. Bruce Catton, *Prefaces to History* (New York: Doubleday, 1970), 96.

14. Roy P. Basler, Marion Dolores Pratt, and Lloyd A. Dunlap, eds., *Collected Works of Abraham Lincoln,* 9 vols. (New Brunswick, N.J.: Rutgers University Press, 1953–55), 3:145.

15. Bell Irwin Wiley, *The Road to Appomattox* (Memphis, Tenn.: Memphis State College Press, 1956), 102.

16. Warren, *Legacy,* 8.

17. Ibid., 83.

18. Stampp, *Imperiled Union*, 255–56.

19. Beringer et al., *Why the South Lost the Civil War*, 76.

20. James M. McPherson, *Ordeal by Fire* (New York: Knopf, 1982), 476.

21. Stampp, *Imperiled Union*, 268.

22. Robert F. Durden, *The Gray and the Black* (Baton Rouge: Louisiana State University Press, 1972), 3.

23. James L. Roark, *Masters without Slaves: Southern Planters in the Civil War and Reconstruction* (New York: Norton, 1977), 105.

24. Dudley Taylor Cornish, *The Sable Arm* (New York: Norton, 1966), 288. Cornish estimates that black soldiers made up between 9 and 10 percent of the total number of Federal soldiers.

25. Thomas J. Pressly, *Americans Interpret Their Civil War* (Princeton: Princeton University Press, 1962).

26. Foster, *Ghosts*, 198; Piston, *Lee's Tarnished Lieutenant*, 157.

27. Fanny Downing, "Perfect through Suffering," *The Land We Love* 4 (January 1868): 193–205.

28. Rev. J. William Jones, *Army of Northern Virginia Memorial Volume* (Richmond: Randolph and English, 1880), 122.

29. Sir Frederick Maurice, *Robert E. Lee the Soldier* (Boston: Houghton Mifflin, 1925), 17.

30. Rev. John Leyburn, "An Interview with Gen. Robert E. Lee," *Century Illustrated Monthly Magazine* 30 (May 1885): 166–67.

31. Gamaliel Bradford, *Lee the American* (Boston: Houghton Mifflin, 1912), 43–44.

32. Douglas Southall Freeman, *R. E. Lee*, 4 vols. (New York: Charles Scribner's Sons, 1942–44), 3:544.

33. Douglas Southall Freeman, *The South to Posterity* (New York: Charles Scribner's Sons, 1951), x, xi.

34. Capt. Robert E. Lee, *Recollections and Letters of Gen. Robert E. Lee* (Garden City, N.Y.: Doubleday, Page, 1924), 25–27.

35. Clifford Dowdey and Louis H. Manarin, eds., *The Wartime Papers of R. E. Lee* (Boston: Little, Brown, 1961), 816; J. F. C. Fuller, *The Generalship of U. S. Grant* (Bloomington: Indiana University Press, 1958), 377.

36. Manfred Weidhorn, *Robert E. Lee* (New York: Atheneum, 1988), 105, 120.

37. Dowdey and Manarin, eds., *Wartime Papers*, 91, 142, 559, 646, 829, 678. *The War of the Rebellion: A Compilation of the Official Records of the Union and Confederate Armies* (Washington, D.C.: U.S. Government Printing Office, 1880–1901), ser. 1, vol. 6, pp. 42–43.

38. *War of the Rebellion*, ser. 1, vol. 46, pt. 3, p. 744; pt. 1, p. 1267.

39. Lee, *Recollections and Letters*, 168.

40. Ibid., 306.

41. Charles Bracelen Flood, *Lee: The Last Years* (Boston: Houghton Mifflin, 1981), 186.

42. W. G. Bean, ed. "Memorandum of Conversations between Robert E. Lee and William Preston Johnson, May 7, 1868 and March 18, 1870," *Virginia Magazine of History and Biography* 73 (October 1965): 477.

43. In the *New York Times Book Review,* July 7, 1991, Faust wrote, "Just as we have distorted the figure of Lee, so we as a nation have remembered the Civil War not as history but as legend. . . . The representation of a Christ-like Lee, free from blemish and uncontaminated by either positive sentiments about slavery or negative feelings about Yankees, provided a myth around which Americans could unite. This in turn became the foundation for a larger legend that discounted slavery as a cause of Southern secession, and led Americans to embrace a racist view of the war that relegated blacks to passive and irrelevant roles and 'deprived . . . the nation as a whole of any high purpose for the war.'"

In the *Journal of Interdisciplinary History* (23 [Summer 1992]: 205–6), McFeely wrote, "The key word in Nolan's book is 'consequence.' One needs to look at what was or would have been the result of a person's actions, particularly when facing a war in which 600,000 of that person's countrymen were killed. The pose of a valorous persona riding above responsibility may work in myth, but not in history. The consequence of successful secession and of fighting the North to a draw or to victory would have meant the preservation of slavery; the consequence of prolonging the war into April 1865 produced more and more deaths and destruction in the South; the consequence of a paternalistic call for conciliation led to the white-people-only reconciliation that did take place.

". . . To honor Lee was to embrace the amnesia with which a whole nation turned its back on the people the war was all about. . . . White America did not want to remember that their black countrymen had had any part in their own liberation. Nor did the nation choose to notice that slavery, for the eradication of which African Americans were supposed to be eternally and quietly grateful, had been replaced by suppression."

44. Marshall W. Fishwick, *Lee after the War* (New York: Dodd, Mead, 1963), 104, 105, 228.

45. Flood, *Lee,* 200

Ulysses S. Grant, October 1861, in a rare image of him dressed in his regulation uniform. This photograph is discussed on page 55, below. Courtesy Library of Congress.

Forging a Commander:
Ulysses S. Grant Enters the Civil War

John Y. Simon

IN THE FALL OF 1990, General H. Norman Schwarzkopf took command of allied forces massing in Saudi Arabia as Operation Desert Shield. Within months, Schwarzkopf, previously little known, achieved widespread fame and recognition for defeating Iraq and liberating Kuwait. A short time later, at the peak of his career, to considerable public mystification and disappointment, Schwarzkopf announced plans for retirement. Yet he had only followed modern bureaucratic systems that impose rigid patterns of age cohorts at levels of responsibility.

Aged fifty-six when he took command in Saudi Arabia, Schwarzkopf had survived a rigorous selection and weeding process in the Department of Defense. Retirements both voluntary and involuntary shaped a pyramid of age and rank that brought major responsibility only to those with the combined qualifications of perceived vigor and experience. At the end of 1990, only 1.6 percent of all officers were older than fifty.[1]

Such expectations of age and leadership, however, do not correlate consistently with historical patterns of age and achievement. At the conclusion of the American Civil War, fifty-eight-year-old Robert E. Lee surrendered to forty-three-year-old Ulysses S. Grant.

Colonel Lee followed Virginia into the Confederacy after declining an offer of top command in the U.S. Army. His admirable military career made such an offer inevitable. In contrast, Grant was then a clerk in his father's leather goods store in Galena, Illinois, in which his younger brother, Orvil, held more authority.

Grant's rapid rise to command originated under wartime conditions that disrupted traditional practices in the seniority system of the old army. Many high-ranking prewar officers, however skilled in administration and strategic planning, were too old to command troops in battle. This situation opened opportunity to potential field commanders outside the military caste system. Grant's comparative youth, combined with his ambivalence toward military orthodoxy, contributed to the amazing self-assurance and audacity that he displayed during the first year of war. Younger than Grant, and lacking his clarity of thought and maturity of judgment, George B. McClellan cowered before an outnumbered foe. His early command of the Army of the Potomac, which carried the dual responsibility of protecting the nation's capital and engaging an enemy army, provided no latitude for experimentation or learning through error. Grant later recognized that he had been more fortunate than McClellan, who had not received the benefit of an apprenticeship in command. Yet good fortune alone could not begin to explain Grant's success. He had seized military opportunities and, even more importantly, had responded effectively to adversity. Within one year after leaving Galena, Grant had exhibited generalship essential to Northern victory.

Command Structure and the Outbreak of War

The U.S. Army provided retirement benefits only for disability.[2] General in Chief Winfield Scott became a general at age twenty-seven during the War of 1812 and held top command in the Mexican War. He had reached the age of seventy-five in 1861, was too heavy to mount a horse, and often dozed at meetings. His incapacity for field duty opened operational command to some younger officer who appeared to possess capacity.

When war began, Quartermaster Joseph E. Johnston, the only general in the U.S. Army young enough to serve in the field, soon resigned to serve the Confederacy. Of the older generals, David E. Twiggs surrendered his forces in Texas quickly enough to raise questions about his loyalty, and William S. Harney lost command after negotiating with secessionists in Missouri. Only John E. Wool served in the field before retiring in 1863. Scott developed an anaconda plan to crush the rebellion by blockading Southern ports, cutting the Confederacy in half by a Mississippi River campaign, then applying steady pressure to the eastern half. Although it was widely ridiculed, in retrospect Scott's plan closely resembled the North's eventual successful strategy. As Major General Irvin McDowell prepared to advance against Richmond in the summer of 1861, Scott urged that the untrained volunteers stand on the defensive since the attacking force would lose. Scott thus accurately predicted the outcome of the Battle of Bull Run. In November 1861, however, after McClellan complained incessantly about Scott's incapacity, the old hero was shipped off to West Point, an early beneficiary of an army retirement law passed in July, perhaps with him in mind. Abraham Lincoln no longer had the benefit of Scott's advice. Instead, the general wrote his *Memoirs*. He sent a copy to Grant graciously inscribed "from the oldest to the ablest General in the world."[3] Perhaps Scott forgot that Wool was two years his senior.

Instead of expanding the small prewar army to accommodate the hundreds of thousands of volunteers needed to suppress the rebellion, the United States created a parallel volunteer force with ranks extending to major general. Generals were nominated by the president and confirmed by the Senate. Their numbers included regular army officers, former regular officers, volunteer officers from the Mexican War, and men appointed for a variety of political reasons, especially prominent Democrats chosen to dramatize that the war was no Republican undertaking. Wartime leadership opened to talent representing a wide range of age, background, and previous rank. Political considerations gave the army such inappropriate generals as Democrat Benjamin F. Butler and Republican Nathaniel P. Banks, both responsible for major Union disasters, but this system also offered leaders like Grant and William T. Sherman the opportunity to display their abilities.

A series of retirements, resignations, and reassignments, combined with a new volunteer army, liberated the United States from the burdens of seniority in field command. Free to create an entirely new force, the Confederacy had no such burden but had elected as president a West Pointer, regular officer, and former secretary of war. Jefferson Davis favored promising talent of the old army. The Confederacy paid dearly for Albert Sidney Johnston, Leonidas Polk, and especially Braxton Bragg.

Besides officers of varied background, the armies had generals of varied ages. Lee's commanders included both his son, Custis, and his nephew, Fitzhugh Lee. Early in the war J. E. B. Stuart's cavalry opposed Union horsemen led by his father-in-law, Philip St. George Cooke. At the close of the war, the U.S. Army's array of twenty-six-year-old commanders included George A. Custer, Nelson A. Miles, and Emory Upton. James Harrison Wilson, twenty-eight years old, commanded the cavalry forces that captured Jefferson Davis. Confederate generals under age thirty included Robert F. Hoke, Evander Law, Stephen Ramseur, Thomas Rosser, Joseph Wheeler, and many others less well known.

One year into the war, the average age of Southern commanders slightly exceeded that of their Northern counterparts.[4] Before the end of the war, despite Lee's brilliant generalship and the disastrous career of young John B. Hood, commanders under fifty had won more major battles than their seniors.[5] Broad surveys of warfare revealed that commanders between forty and forty-five led most armies and that success in battle correlated with closeness in age to forty-five.[6] A subjective survey placed the "zenith" of generalship at age 40.36.[7]

Ulysses S. Grant in the First Year of the Civil War

If destined for fame, Grant showed little prominence on his thirty-ninth birthday, fifteen days after the war began. He had arrived in Springfield, Illinois, the previous evening, escorting a company of Jo Daviess Guards, volunteers raised near his home in Galena. Although he had helped to recruit and train the men, he refused election as captain, believing that his previous military experience qualified him for higher command.[8]

Grant's fifteen years in the army, including four at West Point, brought him the rank of captain when he resigned in 1854. His rank reflected the seniority system of the regular army rather than his ability. No member of his West Point class held higher rank in 1854, and none remaining in service achieved promotion to major before the Civil War. Promotion required the death or resignation of an officer higher in rank, neither a frequent occurrence in peacetime. Junior officers including McClellan, Ambrose E. Burnside, William S. Rosecrans, and Sherman had all resigned from the old army in search of more rewarding careers. Because resignation represented such an attractive alternative to officers blocked in a stagnant seniority system, speculation that Grant drank himself out of the army becomes irrelevant. One who spread such gossip, Captain Henry W. Halleck, resigned the day after Grant did.

Once his recruits reached Springfield, Grant expected to go home, but Congressman Elihu B. Washburne, Grant's fellow townsman, persuaded him to stay to help Governor Richard Yates cope with military paperwork. A few days later, Grant wrote that his "occupation" was "principally smoking and occationally giving advice as to how an order should be communicated."[9] After he traveled to Mattoon, Belleville, and Anna, Illinois, to muster in regiments, his state had no further work for him. In search of a command, he went to St. Louis, then to Cincinnati, where Major General McClellan let Grant sit in the waiting room until he finally gave up. A letter to the federal adjutant general offering Grant's services languished unanswered in War Department files.

Grant received no formal command for two months after the beginning of the Civil War largely because confusion and political manipulation suffused the volunteer army. Ambitious local politicians parlayed recruiting into commissions. Simon S. Goode, who wore a bowie knife and three revolvers, made flamboyant speeches, frequently quoted Napoleon, and claimed never to sleep.[10] Goode initially impressed farm boys from central Illinois and commanded the regiment that Grant had mustered in at Mattoon, but the soldiers soon saw through Goode and ridiculed him into resignation. Needing a firm professional disciplinarian to restore order, Governor Yates remembered Grant.

Had Goode evinced the slightest competence, Grant would not have succeeded to regimental command; now his colonelcy qualified him for advancement to brigadier general. Congressman Washburne caucused with the Illinois delegation and determined the state's fair share of patronage. Entitled to name a brigadier general, Washburne had no better candidate from his district than Grant.[11] Meanwhile, Grant had restored order in his regiment and taken it into north Missouri but had not yet engaged the enemy. How could Grant best explain his military career? "'Man proposes and God disposes.' There are but few important events in the affairs of men brought about by their own choice."[12]

Grant had not chosen military life. His father forced him to attend West Point because the academy provided an excellent education at public expense. Grant remembered his years at West Point as "the most trying days in my life,"[13] later hoped to become a teacher rather than an officer, objected to the Mexican War, and left the army to become a farmer. When duty and responsibility forced him into Civil War service, his ambivalence toward the military gave him perspective. As a professional soldier, he knew the rules yet regarded formal procedure with detachment. Intending to drill his regiment in tactics, Grant studied William J. Hardee's text, drew his regiment in line, and realized that he would first have to raze the houses and gardens of suburban Mexico, Missouri, to make room for standard drill.[14] Grant then literally closed the book on the military thought of the day.

In October 1861, wearing the regulation uniform of a brigadier general, including three black ostrich plumes in his hat, Grant sat for a photographer. An ornamental sword lay across his lap. Perhaps he appeared in full dress to prove to his family that he was a general. It was his first and nearly last appearance in regulation garb. Photographed frequently afterward, he rarely displayed weapons, regulation uniform, or any signs of rank beyond the requisite shoulder stars. Grant was simply too unmilitary to dress like a proper officer.

Ordered to attack the enemy at Florida, Missouri, Colonel Grant led his men to the crest of a hill from which he expected to see his adversaries arrayed for battle. As he advanced, "my heart kept getting higher and higher, until it felt to me as though it was in my throat." He found, however, that the rebels had gone and realized that the enemy "had been as much afraid of me as I had been of him," something he remembered throughout the war.[15]

Grant's subsequent operations demonstrated both self-assurance and considerable audacity. On September 4 he assumed command at Cairo at the tip of Illinois, bordered by hostile Missouri and neutral Kentucky. That day, Confederates violated Kentucky's neutrality by seizing Hickman and Columbus on the Mississippi River. Generals Polk and Gideon J. Pillow had damaged their cause twice over: first by angering wavering Kentuckians seeking to avoid bloodshed in their state and later by failing to make their invasion effective. Grant immediately grasped the opportunity. He informed the Kentucky legislature of the Confederate occupation and telegraphed to his superior, Major General John C. Frémont, at headquarters in St. Louis, for permission to seize Paducah, at the mouth of the Tennessee River.[16]

Frémont telegraphed permission in Hungarian.[17] Surrounded by officers who had fled Hungary after the abortive revolt of 1848, Frémont had decided that their impenetrable language would serve effectively as code. He had already asked Grant to telegraph information about troop dispositions in Hungarian. But if Frémont's authorization to seize Paducah arrived before Grant left, nobody at Cairo could translate the message, and Grant believed that he received permission to seize Paducah only after his forces had returned from their successful expedition. By acting quickly, Grant thought that he had forestalled a Confederate occupation of a vital position.[18] In this belief, he had overestimated Polk and Pillow but had given them no time to rectify their initial blunder.

For the next two months, Grant chafed at his inactivity in Cairo while Frémont displayed his incapacity in St. Louis. Finally, President Lincoln replaced Frémont with Halleck. In the brief interval between Frémont's removal and Halleck's arrival, Grant led an expedition to Belmont, Missouri, a Confederate camp across the Mississippi River from Columbus. He loaded more than 3,000 men on transports and sent a force by land toward Columbus. Landing undetected above Belmont, Grant's army overran the Confederate garrison and pushed it in demoralization to the river. Victorious celebration in Grant's own ranks gave Confederates time to ferry reinforcements across the Mississippi, then drive Grant back to his transports. Both sides later claimed victory without adequate justification.

In his report, Grant sought to base his attack on orders from St. Louis and timely intelligence about Confederate movements.[19] So tangled did his explanations become that staff officers prepared a second report in 1864 that was not transmitted to the War Department until after the war ended. Beneath the smoke lay the reality: whatever Frémont or Confederates had intended, Grant planned to attack at Belmont and did so without authorization from headquarters.

Once Halleck took command, order and caution ruled under a military professional whom Grant respected. Grant turned his attention to the Tennessee River, which was guarded by Fort Henry. The Confederates built Fort Henry in Tennessee during Kentucky's neutrality, locating the fort as close as possible to Kentucky. But engineers selected a site too low for effective defense when the river rose, and at St. Louis and near Cairo the North built gunboats that the South could not counter. Grant asked Halleck for authority to lead a combined army-navy expedition against Fort Henry, persisting until Halleck reluctantly assented.

The capture of Fort Henry was something of an anticlimax. With much of its defensive capability sapped by high water, the fort surrendered to the gunboats before most of the troops arrived. Much of the garrison fled about eleven miles to the east to Fort Donelson on the Cumberland River, a far larger and stronger position. Grant immediately planned to march to Fort Donelson, telegraphing his plans to Halleck and sending gunboats down the Tennessee so that they could ascend the Cumberland.[20]

Halleck's reaction to Grant's plan for a campaign against Fort Donelson was a model of military bureaucracy. In communicating with Grant, Halleck gave no clue that he knew anything about Grant's expedition. If successful, Halleck intended to claim all credit; if unsuccessful, he would take no responsibility. Grant himself became too absorbed in moving his army to heed the silence from St. Louis.

Grant knew his adversaries. Former Secretary of War John B. Floyd commanded, with Pillow second in command and likely to lead field operations. Only Simon B. Buckner, third in rank, had any military competence. Expecting little opposition en route to Donelson, Grant sent his army on two different roads and, on arrival, encircled the Confederate garrison of 21,000 with his own army of 15,000. He awaited the arrival of gunboats and additional federal troops, which ultimately increased his numbers to 27,000. On February 14, the gunboats shelled the water batteries, came too close, and suffered losses that crippled the fleet and wounded its commander, Andrew H. Foote.

While Grant consulted with Foote on his flagship the next morning, Pillow launched an attack on the Union right, rolling it back to the center and opening a line of retreat to Nashville. Pillow seemed so surprised by his victory that he became confused about whether to press the attack or to evacuate the garrison. When Grant returned, he rallied his troops and counterattacked on the left, which Pillow had weakened to assault on the right. Pillow withdrew to his fortifications to consider further his options. The Confederates then decided to surrender. Floyd and Pillow left by steamboat with about 2,000 men, while Nathan Bedford Forrest led his cavalry and a few infantry overland to Nashville. Command finally fell to Buckner after his two seniors had made the situation hopeless. To Buckner's request to appoint commissioners to negotiate terms of capitulation, Grant replied succinctly that "no terms except an unconditional and immediate surrender can be accepted." After Buckner denounced the response as "ungenerous and unchivalrous," he surrendered anyway.[21] Grant captured about 15,000 prisoners and forty-eight artillery pieces. After winning the first significant Union victory of the war, Grant received an immediate promotion to major general.

Even this decisive victory did not give Halleck confidence in Grant. Immediately after the fall of Fort Henry, General in Chief McClellan suggested that Halleck take personal command of the Fort Donelson expedition or give it to Don Carlos Buell. Halleck chose Buell. After Donelson fell, Halleck complained to McClellan that Grant had gone to Nashville without authority, failed to report his strength, and, pleased with victory, "sits down and enjoys it without any regard to the future." More to the point, he reported a rumor that Grant had "resumed his former bad habits." Halleck reported accurately but misleadingly that Charles F. Smith, "by his coolness and bravery at Fort Donelson when the battle was against us, turned the tide and carried the enemy's outworks."[22] Authorized by McClellan to place Grant under arrest, Halleck instead ordered him to remain at Fort Henry while Smith commanded the Tennessee River expedition headed toward Corinth, Mississippi. Three times in one week Grant asked to be relieved. Halleck backed down.

Which of this flurry of charges Halleck truly believed remains unclear. The success of a self-assured and audacious junior officer undoubtedly galled Halleck, perhaps awakening suspicions that Grant might eventually become his superior, which Grant did two years later. An officer who went by the book—Halleck had written a book—resented one who threw it away. Grant would have sympathized with Halleck's preference for Smith. Like his fellow West Point cadets, young Grant had admired Commandant Smith—tall, handsome, and militarily correct in deportment. Smith then proved his mettle in Mexico, and Grant found it embarrassing to command an officer whom he so respected. Fifty-four years old, Smith looked and acted like a commander. Ultimately, however, Halleck could not follow his instincts without sound charges against the victor at Fort Donelson.

Restored to command, Grant shipped his army to Pittsburg Landing for the overland campaign against Corinth. At his headquarters at Savannah, Tennessee, nine miles away, he awakened to the guns of Shiloh. Preparing to attack Albert Sidney Johnston at Corinth, he never suspected that the Confederate general would attack him. Encouraged by Sherman, Grant ignored all warning signs. On April 6, his army suffered a disastrous defeat as Confederates broke through the lines and pushed the demoralized army to the banks of the Tennessee. The next day, aided by reinforcements, Grant counterattacked vigorously and regained the field, sending his foe back to Corinth with heavy losses. For the two-day battle, losses staggered both sides. Reacting as if to defeat, Halleck finally left St. Louis to take charge, giving Grant only a nominal role as second in command.

During the battle of Shiloh, Smith lay bedridden at Savannah. He had scraped his leg while jumping into a boat, and infection followed. When he died on April 25, Grant expressed "heartfelt grief."[23]

Had Smith been healthy, he probably would have succeeded Grant in command while Halleck remained at his desk.

On his thirty-ninth birthday, Grant was a clerk; on his fortieth birthday, April 27, 1862, Grant was a major general who had fought three important battles, two of them smashing victories. He had lost three contests: he had been swept from the field at Belmont, Pillow had broken his lines at Donelson, and Confederates had won the first day at Shiloh. On the last two occasions, however, with calm, resolute confidence, he had more than redeemed his losses with a vigorous counterattack.

On his fortieth birthday, Grant might again have reported his occupation as "principally smoking," yet his letters home give no hint of emotion. He was "no longer boss. Gen. Halleck is here and I am truly glad of it." Halleck, was, he thought, "one of the greatest men of the age." "In Gen. Sherman," he wrote of the most truly surprised officer at Shiloh, "the country has an able and gallant defender and your husband a true friend." As to the barrage of newspaper criticism, Grant urged his wife to "give yourself no trouble" as he expected to "come out all right without a single contradiction." He reported himself and staff "all well and me as sober as a deacon no matter what is said to the contrary."[24] Letters home serve as a forceful reminder that Grant was still a young officer learning how to fight the Civil War. He responded to adversity with rare equanimity, was neither elated by victory nor crushed by defeat, and had the clarity of vision to make quick and decisive appraisals of military problems.

George B. McClellan

While Grant developed his talents as a commander in the western theater of war, another young general held command in the east. Following the Union defeat at Bull Run in July 1861, McClellan at age thirty-five took command of the Army of the Potomac. McClellan had graduated second in his West Point class, served as an engineer and observer of the Crimean War, and resigned in 1857 to become chief engineer of the Illinois Central Railroad. Appointed major general of Ohio Volunteers when war began, his operations in western Virginia attracted favorable attention in Washington.

McClellan shared none of Grant's audacity. His experience in western Virginia carried the same lesson Grant had learned in Missouri—the enemy was as afraid of him as he was of the enemy—yet he constantly overestimated the strength and capacity of his opponents. Taking command of a defeated and demoralized force, he recognized that it needed discipline and training but overestimated the time required. Through the summer and fall of 1861 he built an effective army that he refused to lead into the field.[25]

If he did not want to use his army, others did. On October 21, 1861, Senator Edward D. Baker of Oregon led a small force across the Potomac near Leesburg to destroy a Confederate camp falsely reported to be on the opposite bluff. A close friend of Lincoln, who had named one son in his honor, Baker had raised a regiment and hoped for military honors exceeding those he had already won in the Mexican War. First he needed to prove himself in battle. Taking advantage of discretionary orders to create a diversion, he plunged into the disaster at Ball's Bluff, sacrificing his men and losing his own life.

The aftereffects were devastating. Some congressional Republicans blamed McClellan and General Charles P. Stone, Baker's immediate superior. McClellan shifted blame to Winfield Scott, soon hustled into retirement, and McClellan eventually sacrificed Stone, authorizing his imprisonment while fully aware that the punishment was unjust. McClellan knew that Baker bore responsibility for a military blunder but could not openly condemn a fallen hero beloved by the president.

During the winter 1861–62 the price of any potential defeat rose for McClellan. Perhaps he suspected that he might some day occupy a cell in New York Harbor next to Stone. To ensure against disaster, McClellan needed more men. Until they arrived, he needed to avoid battle. He eventually lost all initiative. Responding to

Lincoln's direct order to advance, he marched 112,000 men toward Manassas. On arrival three days later they found only smoldering wreckage of the former Confederate camp; the vastly outnumbered foe had withdrawn. On this day, Lincoln stripped McClellan of his position as general in chief, inherited from Scott, leaving McClellan in command of the Army of the Potomac.

McClellan won grudging approval from Lincoln for his planned advance on Richmond via the peninsula between the York and James Rivers. As he left, however, Lincoln withheld McDowell's Corps to defend the capital, overruling McClellan's protests that he needed those 30,000 troops. McClellan still had 100,000 men to confront an enemy little more than half that number, yet his self-confidence was shattered. Under the circumstances, it is remarkable that McClellan fought the enemy to a standstill, unremarkable that he could not deliver a knockout blow.

On the day Grant reached his fortieth birthday, McClellan besieged Yorktown. John B. Magruder, commanding 10,000 men confronting an army ten times larger, moved his troops from point to point to simulate a larger army and displayed logs painted black to resemble cannons. Completely fooled, McClellan looked on fearfully while Confederates assembled forces from elsewhere in Virginia. To Lincoln's dismay, McClellan ordered heavy artillery to shell what he believed to be formidable lines. McClellan's sound military training and considerable talent were buried under a paralyzing cloud of fear.

Hailed in July 1861 as a young Napoleon, McClellan had indeed shown his youth. Essentially insecure, he had demanded guaranteed success before moving against the enemy. Every setback prompted excuses, and he quickly blamed others for his mistakes as well as their own. Intensely self-conscious, he constantly fretted about what others thought of him, and this concern extended beyond his troops to the entire Northern population.

The spotlight fell on McClellan before he was prepared for a leading role. Under intense scrutiny, he had no opportunity to improvise or to learn from mistakes. His prominence in command gave him an inevitable political dimension, alarming congressional Republicans, who were impatient for action, quick to criticize any Democrat, and unforgiving. At the outset of an unprecedented civil conflict, political and military spheres intersected and collided. In the confusion, the army needed senior management. In retrospect, Scott performed admirably, despite the handicaps of age. With Scott too old and McClellan too young, disproportionate responsibility fell on Lincoln.

When Grant inherited the position of general in chief in early 1864, he thought of tapping the talents of generals shelved too early in the war, including McClellan and Buell. Grant did not press the point, and McClellan had drifted into politics and eventually received the Democratic nomination for president.[26] Years later, McClellan's downfall still troubled Grant: "The two disadvantages under which he labored were his receiving a high command before he was ready for it, and the political sympathies which he allowed himself to champion. It is a severe blow to any one to begin so high. . . . If McClellan had gone into the war as Sherman, Thomas, or Meade, had fought his way along and up, I have no reason to suppose that he would not have won as high a distinction as any of us."[27] And why not? Although McClellan possessed serious character flaws, he had no opportunity to learn through experimentation and adversity. He was, after all, still young.

Conclusion

"A successful general needs health and youth and energy," mused Grant. "I should not like to put a general in the field over fifty. . . . The power to endure is an immense power, and naturally belongs to youth."[28] Grant considered Lee too old for field command, as perhaps he was late in the war after his health deteriorated.[29] Yet Lee was hardly the example to prove the point; neither was McClellan.

Grant seemed at a loss to explain his success in the Civil War. Age furnished part of the equation, giving him the vigor and energy to operate effectively when deprived of sleep or food, to think clearly when beset with detail and clamor. The broad perspective in which he thought, however, stemmed from something else. Versatility and flexibility marked his reactions to military problems. Unlike officers well trained in the art of war, he reacted to military situations with logic rather than formula.

Good luck certainly contributed to Grant's success, especially early in the war. Because he lived in Galena he received the patronage of a powerful Republican congressman. Circumstance placed him at Cairo at the precise moment that Confederates under Polk and Pillow violated Kentucky's neutrality. On his expedition to Belmont he encountered forces commanded by the same two generals, and Pillow reappeared at Fort Donelson. After hammering Grant at Shiloh, General Albert Sidney Johnston fell in battle. Sherman believed that "had C. F. Smith lived, Grant would have disappeared to history after Donelson."[30]

Grant had bad luck also. Untrained volunteers at Belmont, led by politically appointed colonels, got out of hand and permitted Confederates to regroup. Pillow struck at Donelson just as Grant conferred miles away with his wounded naval counterpart. Subordinates at Shiloh, who failed to scout adequately, ignored warnings of impending attack. Both Grant's immediate superior, Halleck, and Halleck's superior, McClellan, distrusted Grant's character and ability.

Chance and contingency play such powerful roles in complex human careers that cataloging examples of good or bad fortune cannot yield worthwhile results. Grant's success during the first year of the Civil War hinged primarily upon his seizure of opportunities and his effective response to adversity. For an officer under forty, these qualities combined maturity of judgment with youthful resilience and versatility. Grant responded to battlefield confusion without emotion. Only four years in age separated McClellan and Grant, yet the psychological gap was immense. Historians contemplating the Civil War must conclude that McClellan was the architect of his failure, Grant the architect of his success.

Only militaristic nations enter war fully prepared for com-

bat. The military establishment of the United States, unprepared for an enemy with substantial strength, went into the Civil War with an officer corps rusted with disuse and shattered by defection. A generation earlier, Alexis de Tocqueville predicted that "great generals are always sure to spring up. A long war produces upon a democratic army the same effects that a revolution produces upon a people; it breaks through regulations and allows extraordinary men to rise above the common level."[31] Youth, obscurity, and inexperience remained handicaps in the Civil War, but they were more readily overcome than the burdens of tradition. As Grant put it, "The laws of successful war in one generation would insure defeat in another."[32] Grant learned this lesson in battle long before he articulated the thought. Discovering methods of winning Civil War battles under fire constituted a continuing process of forging a commander.

Notes

1. *Defense* 91 (September–October 1991): 28.

2. John S. McNeil, Pedro J. Lecca, and Roosevelt Wright, Jr., *Military Retirement: Social, Economic, and Mental Health Dilemmas* (Totowa, N.J.: Rowman and Allanheld, 1983), 5–6.

3. *New York Herald*, November 22, 1864.

4. Herman Hattaway and Archer Jones, *How the North Won: A Military History of the Civil War* (Urbana: University of Illinois Press, 1983), 502.

5. John Y. Simon and Gunnar Boalt, "Losses in War: A Sociological Approach," in Boalt, *Competing Belief Systems* (Stockholm: Almqvist and Wiksell International, 1984).

6. Harvey C. Lehman, *Age and Achievement* (Princeton: Princeton University Press, 1953), 170; Dean Keith Simonton, "Land Battles, Generals, and Armies: Individual and Situational Determinants of Success," *Journal of Personality and Social Psychology* 38 (1980): 114–16.

7. J. F. C. Fuller, *Generalship: Its Diseases and Their Cure* (Harrisburg, Pa.: Military Service Publishing, 1936), 97; see Fuller, *The Generalship of Ulysses S. Grant* (New York: Dodd, Mead, 1929), 5.

8. Ulysses S. Grant, *Personal Memoirs of U. S. Grant* (New York: Charles L. Webster, 1885–86), 1:231–41.

9. Ulysses S. Grant to Julia Dent Grant, May 1, 1861, in John Y. Simon,

ed., *The Papers of Ulysses S. Grant* (Carbondale and Edwardsville: Southern Illinois University Press, 1967–), 2:16.

10. Hamlin Garland, *Ulysses S. Grant: His Life and Character* (New York: Macmillan, 1920), 165–66.

11. Theodore Calvin Pease and James G. Randall, eds., *The Diary of Orville Hickman Browning* (Springfield: Illinois State Historical Library, 1925), 1:487–88, 490; James Harrison Wilson, *The Life of John A. Rawlins* (New York: Neale, 1916), 52–53.

12. Grant, *Memoirs,* 1:[7].

13. John Russell Young, *Around the World with General Grant* (New York: American News, 1879), 2:450.

14. Grant, *Memoirs,* 1:253.

15. Ibid., 1:250.

16. Grant to Frémont, September 5, 1861, in Simon, ed., *Papers,* 2:190.

17. Frémont to Grant, September 5, 1861, ibid., 2:191–92.

18. Grant, *Memoirs,* 1:265–66.

19. Grant to Seth Williams, November 10, 17, 1861, in Simon, ed., *Papers,* 3:141–52.

20. Grant to John C. Kelton, February 6, 1862, to George C. Cullum, February 8, 1862, to Halleck, February 13, 1862, all ibid., 4:157, 172, 195.

21. Grant to Buckner, February 16, 1862, Buckner to Grant, February 16, 1862, ibid., 4:218.

22. Halleck to McClellan, March 3, 4, 1862, February 19, 1862, all in *The War of the Rebellion: A Compilation of the Official Records of the Union and Confederate Armies* (Washington, D.C.: U.S. Government Printing Office, 1880–1901), ser. 1, vol. 7, pp. 679–80, 682, 637.

23. Grant to Mrs. Charles F. Smith, April 26, 1862, in Simon, ed., *Papers,* 5:84.

24. Grant to Julia Dent Grant, April 25, 30, May 4, 13, 1862, ibid., 5:72, 102, 103, 110, 111, 118.

25. Stephen W. Sears, *George B. McClellan: The Young Napoleon* (New York: Ticknor and Fields, 1988).

26. Grant, *Memoirs,* 2:119–21; Young, *Around the World,* 2:445; James B. Fry, *Operations of the Army under Buell* (New York: Van Nostrand, 1884), 200–201.

27. Young, *Around the World,* 2:463, 217.

28. Ibid., 2:353.

29. Ibid., 2:459–60.

30. William Tecumseh Sherman to Robert N. Scott, September 6, 1885, in Sherman, "An Unspoken Address to the Loyal Legion," *North American*

Review 142 (March 1886): 302–3. Quoted in James B. Fry, "An Acquaintance with Grant," *North American Review* 141 (December 1885): 551. Sherman originally attempted to deny that he had written this letter. Allen Thorndike Rice, "Sherman on Grant," *North American Review* 142 (January 1886): 111–13; Rice, "Sherman's Opinion of Grant," *North American Review* 142 (February 1886): 200–208. See *New York Times*, January 30, February 19, 1886.

    31. Alexis de Tocqueville, *Democracy in America* (New York: Knopf, 1945), 2:278.

    32. Young, *Around the World*, 2:625.

Thomas "Stonewall" Jackson, 1855, while on the faculty of Virginia Military Institute. Courtesy National Portrait Gallery, Smithsonian Institution.

Stonewall Jackson:
A "Pious, Blue-Eyed Killer?"

James I. Robertson, Jr.

NOT TOO LONG AGO, professional historians of the Civil War period thought that they controlled the impact and the legacy of that struggle. But those who toil in the Civil War vineyard are rapidly finding that the war controls them, shaping their activities as completely as it did those of its participants. The magnetism of the American war draws us together to examine the incredible fascination inherent in that conflict.

A partial explanation for such unprecedented infatuation lies in a statement made by Walker Percy. In 1957 he noted, "The truth of it is, I think, that the whole country . . . is just beginning to see the Civil War whole and entire for the first time. The thing was too big and too bloody, too full of suffering and hatred, too closely knit into the fabric of our meaning as a people, to be held off and looked at— until now. It is like a man walking away from a mountain. The bigger it is, the farther he's got to go before he can see it. Then one day he looks back and there it is, this colossal thing lying across his past."[1]

That mountain occupies our thoughts; human aspects of it command our attention. My task, a pleasant one indeed, is to share some thoughts about Stonewall Jackson, a man who has been a lifelong companion.

He is certainly not the man whom Ken Burns's *Civil War* categorized as "a pious, blue-eyed killer." Of course, the less one knows about the Civil War, the more one likes Burns's production. The portrayal of General Stonewall Jackson is a sad illustration of the series' sometimes vain search for accuracy.

As an example: a photograph appears on the screen as a purported likeness of Jackson. The figure is smiling and grossly overweight—two characteristics that would have surprised anyone who ever saw the Confederate general.

Again: for the May 25, 1862, battle of Winchester, Virginia, a map depicts Jackson attacking the city from the north. The befuddled Union commander, Nathaniel P. Banks, would believe this hypothesis because he was convinced that Jackson was striking from every direction. In actuality, the Confederate assault came from the south.

It does seem unfair to dismiss Jackson as a pious, blue-eyed killer without labeling William T. Sherman an agnostic, redheaded psychopath. But enough name-calling. Let us instead talk of charisma.

Webster gives two definitions of the word. In Christian theology, charisma is "a divinely inspired gift, grace, or talent." The more popular definition of charisma is "a special quality of leadership that captures the popular imagination and inspires allegiance and devotion." General Thomas Jonathan Jackson would have endorsed the first meaning. Posterity remembers him by the second.

He made little or no impression in the first days of civil war. Oblivious to dress, he was recognizable by his seediness. Jackson even sat a horse awkwardly, body bent far forward as if leaning into a stiff wind.[2] He was known for his silence rather than for any utterances; he gave little appearance of ability, much less of genius.

Unheralded in the spring of 1861, his first assignment was to command the Harpers Ferry post where eager young recruits were gathering. Jackson's performance was solid if unspectacular. Conversely, his first battle—near Manassas, Virginia, and along Bull Run—was so creditable that the most famous nickname in the war emerged. Thereafter, he was Stonewall Jackson to friend and foe. (The nickname was a misnomer. Alert, energetic, a master of quick military movement, Jackson merited his famous sobriquet only in that his large frame and determined air gave him a rocklike firmness.)

The following spring, he electrified military circles around the world with an audacious campaign in Virginia's Shenandoah Valley. Jackson's boldness resulted in the most brilliant Confederate success of the war to that point. The little-known college professor had saved Richmond from quick capture, disrupted all Union plans for operations in Virginia, and defeated three separate enemy armies that together outnumbered his forces by four to one. In addition, Jackson insured the safety of the valley, inflicted 7,000 casualties at a cost of fewer than half that number, seized 9,000 small arms, and confiscated tons of badly needed arms and stores.

General Richard B. Ewell was Jackson's second in command during the activities in the valley. At the end of the campaign, someone asked Ewell to evaluate Jackson's performance. The crusty subaltern snorted, "Well, sir, when he commenced it I thought him crazy; when he ended it I thought him inspired."[3]

Within a year, "Old Jack" (as his men called him) became the foremost hero in the Southern Confederacy. In European eyes, he stood as the most spectacular soldier of the Civil War. Time did little to dim that reputation. Lord Roberts, who served as commander in chief of the British armies in India, Ireland, and South Africa in the late nineteenth century, observed, "In my opinion Stonewall Jackson was one of the greatest natural military geniuses the world ever saw. I will go even further than that—as a campaigner in the field he never had a superior. In some respects I doubt whether he ever had an equal."[4]

After the 1862 Shenandoah Valley campaign, and certainly following victory in the Second Manassas campaign, Jackson became the idol of the South. When he passed through towns, people would pour into the streets to see him. Mothers would come to him with children in their arms to ask for his blessing upon the infants. If they could not get close enough, the mothers at least could later remind their children that they were once in the presence of the immortal Jackson.

The same adoration existed inside the ranks of his corps. Captain

Hugh White of Lexington wrote home in the summer of 1862, "There is but one feeling with us—that of perfect devotion to Gen. Jackson. With him we are ready to go anywhere, and to endure anything."[5] White did exactly that: he was killed in action a few days later.

Another Virginia soldier was as lavish in his praise. "There was something about Jackson that always attracted his men," Sergeant John H. Worsham recalled. "It must have been faith. He was the idol of his soldiers. . . . The very sight of him was the signal for cheers. It made no difference where he was—in camp, on the battlefield, or on a march; when the men were so thoroughly used up that they could hardly put one foot before the other, or when they were lying down resting on the roadside, the sight of Jackson riding by caused each man to jump to his feet, pull off his hat, and cheer him." Worsham added, "The South produced many generals of great ability; but for brilliancy and dash, the world never saw Stonewall Jackson's equal."[6]

Such feelings were not confined to the Southern states. Near the end of 1862, U.S. Congressman Daniel W. Voorhees of Indiana supposedly acknowledged publicly that Jackson was the only man who could beat him in an election in his Hoosier district.[7]

Such respect and affection exist in scores of wartime chronicles, which is remarkable in light of the fact that Jackson died at the midway point of the Civil War, after barely two years in the field. In just twenty-two months, he attained a fame unparalleled for that time.

But the mystery surrounding Jackson is much broader. For a century and a half, writers have sought answers, created myths, and suggested absurdities in an effort to explain this orphan who seemingly matured into an enigma. On the surface, Jackson appeared to be a strange mixture of contrasts: restlessness and repose, complexity and simplicity, hardness and softness, eccentricity and excellence, ambition and humility, wrathfulness and righteousness. Steadily through those incompatible qualities emerged a wondrous charisma that has transcended the ages.

What is this magnetism that still attracts serious students of the Civil War? For one thing, the words Jackson used so often—*faith, duty, devotion, honor*—have a quaint sound in our age because they are unfamiliar. Cynics sneer today that no one like Jackson could have existed, but only because no one like Jackson exists now. An old proverb says that the mountain is a mystery when one looks only at the ground. If we have grown incapable of lifting our heads and viewing the heights—if, in other words, we have grown callous to the inspiration of heroes, that says something about us, not them.

Jackson defies normal analysis for another reason. Military genius and religious devotion are uncommon traits. When one individual possesses both of these contrasting assets, he stands alone on a high pedestal that is extraordinary to some viewers, enigmatic to others. Major David Boyd, a commissary officer under Jackson, noted that both Sherman and Jackson were considered mentally unbalanced in the first year of the Civil War: "Nobody seemed to understand [Jackson]. But so it has been and ever will be: when we ordinary mortals can't comprehend a genius, we get even with him by calling him crazy."[8]

It is also important to bear in mind that Jackson is difficult to understand because he lived in another time—a time that has little in common with life in the closing years of the twentieth century. To study Jackson, to see clearly the man that he was (and not the ambitious buffoon or cold-blooded killer that some writers addicted to sensationalism have manufactured), one must pursue the first commandment for a graduate student in history: "Thou shalt look at the past through the lenses of the past and not through the distorting mirrors of the present."

History is not the past but the present's account of the past. Those who worship "historical revisionism" are being redundant, for every new work revises the past in the light (or, so often, in the darkness) of the present. It is a familiar conceit of historians that they, and only they, see reality. In actuality, they see the first reflection of their own times and their own prejudices.

Many people go wrong in the field of history by failing to see that historical figures did not have 130 years to reflect on their actions or their utterances. Hindsight, like sugar, is palatable when used with moderation. One should not measure minutely the events of the past on the scales of the present. Such an approach is at least misleading and at most foolish.

In spite of such machinations, charisma still swirls around Stonewall Jackson. One of its foundations is military leadership. Jackson swept into war subtly but with cool professionalism. He accepted authority with confidence in himself, with a sense of discipline, and with the profound conviction that the war would be a tough contest for the South. Lighthearted enthusiasm, the opportunity for glory, the eagerness of youth, were not in his makeup. Jackson saw war as the Old Testament portrayed it: grim, bloody, uncompromising, with a totality demanded by the God of Battle.

Jackson never allowed friendship or human feelings to stand in the way of duty. He drilled his troops constantly. Discipline was ever present and severe. His soldiers marched, marched, and marched even more. They set an incredibly rapid pace in both speed and endurance that earned them the appellation "foot cavalry." It is also significant that in 1861 Brigadier General Jackson's First Brigade of Virginia acquired pride before it gained experience and the lasting name "Stonewall Brigade." Its members did not always understand Jackson, but they reveled in victory and they trusted their commander.

Unlike most commanders with an inspiring touch, Jackson did not prepare his men for combat with great speeches or lofty words. Nor was he dashing in appearance or outgoing in behavior. Quite the contrary. He was the least ostentatious of commanders. Displays of affection embarrassed him. His soldiers knew his feelings, which was part of the reason they cheered so loudly when he came in sight. Jackson always responded with humility. If galloping past his troops, he respectfully held his hat in his hand as silent acknowledgment of their devotion. He disdained splendid garb and wore his old Virginia Military Institute uniform until it had the shabbiness of reduced gentility. Pomposity was alien to Jackson's makeup, one of his men asserted, because the general was "too absorbed to give thought or time to the subject."[9] That he sought to avoid flattery and praise only enhanced his charisma. To Daniel Harvey Hill he once said, "These newspaper [reports] make me ashamed." On another occasion, responding to a laudatory newspaper account, he declared, "The way in which press, army, and people seem to lean on individuals fills me with alarm. They are forgetting God in his instruments."[10]

Courage under fire and genuine concern for the welfare of his men became part of Jackson's inspirational character. He was cold and determined when pressing his columns forward to meet the enemy. One observer noted, "In fertility of resource, in quickness and boldness of execution, Jackson had no equal. In his terrible marches, he sped over the country like the messenger of Fate—undeterred by difficulties that would have been regarded by others as insuperable."[11]

Jackson always maintained two ironclad beliefs: constant drill was the key to good discipline, and good discipline was the foundation for military supremacy. Jackson himself listed two factors as necessary for military success. First,

> always mystify, mislead, and surprise the enemy if possible; and when you strike and overcome him, never let up in the pursuit so long as your men have strength to follow; for an army routed, if hotly pursued, becomes panic-stricken, and can then be destroyed by half their number.
>
> The other rule is, never fight against heavy odds, if by any possible maneuvering you can hurl your own force on only a part—and that the weakest part—of your enemy and crush it. Such tactics will win every time, and a small army may thus destroy a large one in detail; and repeated victory will make it invincible.[12]

It should be emphasized that Jackson rarely made such prolonged observations. His comments were usually quite succinct. Once, on a long ride, he turned to a member of his staff and asked seriously, "Did it ever occur to you, sir, what an opportunity a battlefield affords liars?"[13]

A supernatural air came to surround Jackson and added to his charisma because he veiled all of his great movements in mystery. Indeed, he masked his designs with elaborate care—sometimes making minute inquiries in regard to roads in one direction and then suddenly striking camp and marching off in the opposite direction. Guides were posted at road junctions to point the line of march. All that division commanders knew at any given time was to lead their brigades down a particular road until a guide somewhere in the distance told them what next to do. Jackson often bivouacked at crossroads to make it impossible for anyone to know which way he might go the next day. Such things led a captain once to shake his head and observe, "If silence is golden, then Jackson is rich indeed!"[14]

Victory promotes charisma, even though the means to that end may be harsh. Robert E. Lee and Stonewall Jackson formed a near-perfect military partnership, yet there was a major difference between the two generals. At times Lee seemed so reluctant to hurt the feelings of subalterns he thought were doing their best that he occasionally permitted incompetents to remain in command. The kindness of his heart occasionally impaired the efficiency of his army. Jackson, in contrast, was stern, remorseless, unforgiving. His goal was to crush the enemy beyond redemption, and if any officer for any reason failed to live up to expectations, Jackson thrust him aside with as little ceremony as if transferring a private to another command.

No form of scandal or immorality marred Jackson's career. His character was as unblemished as Lee's. General James H. Lane, one of Jackson's cadets years before he became one of his brigadiers, stated after the war, "This great soldier was pure and clean as ever man was. . . . Of the slightest equivocation or of any conscious indiscretion he was absolutely incapable." General Basil Duke added that Jackson "possessed in very marked degree the moral qualifications most essential to war."[15]

Jackson gained absolute respect. Sometimes it came swiftly, sometimes it came begrudgingly, the result of his peculiarities and his first impressions. It is unfortunate that those aspects have dominated the picture of Jackson, because they are grossly misleading.

For example, all good students of Confederate military history are familiar with General Richard Taylor's initial encounter with the strange Stonewall. It was early in the 1862 Shenandoah Valley campaign, and Taylor had been sent to report to the Virginian. According to Taylor's memoirs (which, incidentally, never let truth stand in the way of a good story), he found Jackson sitting on a fence, "feet of gigantic size, [wearing] a mangy cap with visor down," and intently sucking a lemon. To Taylor's eager statements, Jackson replied only with grunts and cryptic comments. This image has provided chuckles for generations of Civil War students.

Overlooked because of this colorful first impression is Taylor's ultimate judgment of Jackson forty pages later in his book: "What limit is set to [Jackson's] ability, I know not, for he was ever superior to occasion. . . . [His] peculiarities . . . served to enhance his martial fame. . . . With Wolfe and Nelson and Havelock, he took his place in the hearts of [all] English-speaking peoples." No eccentric character exists in that summation.[16]

Similarly, General Richard Ewell thought Jackson "crazy . . . insane" and asked for transfer to another theater. Two months later, Ewell confessed, "I take it all back, and will never prejudge another man. Old Jackson is no fool; he . . . does curious things, but he has method in his madness."[17] Every general on the Union side supported that assertion.

Jackson had two distinct sides to his personality. One was the bold and determined general in combat. The other was shy, reticent, wedded to duty, unsuccessful as a teacher but demonstrably loving as a husband and drawn with unabashed affection toward every child he ever met. The latter quality also contributed to his charisma.

Most people did not or could not know Jackson. Hence, they tended to jump to quick and false conclusions. His introverted nature gave rise to still other theories. Much of the charisma around Jackson presumably came from his story of "the poor boy who made good"—the saga of an orphan hoping to find an acceptable place in the world and, in the process, searching for the love denied him in his formative years.

Few great leaders have developed from sadder beginnings than did Jackson. His childhood was so full of sorrow that he would not discuss that period of his life. Only his two wives were able to pry the heart-wrenching facts from him.

Born near midnight on January 20, 1824, in the mountainous region of what was then northwestern Virginia, he was the third of four children of a ne'er-do-well attorney. His father and older sister died of typhoid fever when Thomas was two. The young widow and her three children became virtual wards of the town of Clarksburg, where they resided. In 1830 Mrs. Jackson remarried. Her new husband, much older than his bride and of limited means, was unable to care for so many dependents, and the three children were sent to live with relatives. Thomas saw his mother only one more time. In 1831, as she lay dying from a combination of the effects of childbirth and probable tuberculosis, she asked that her seven-year-old son be brought to her for a final visit. The farewell was tearful on the outside, traumatic on the inside. Jackson could never forget the searing memories of that day.

Separated almost entirely from his brother and sister, the withdrawn and lonely youth spent his boyhood years on the farm of a bachelor uncle. Young Tom looked up to his uncle, Cummins Jackson, who was a shrewd businessman, a dominant force in local affairs, a gambler, a hard drinker, and ultimately a counterfeiter who fled west to avoid federal imprisonment. Cummins Jackson gave his nephew the security of a home, but he was incapable of imparting the love an orphaned and lonely child not only craved but needed. What education the boy received came during the winter months and from local tutors. Jackson was always proficient in mathematics; his love of reading enhanced his frontier education. Most of what he learned was self-acquired. He was hardly qualified for a college education; nevertheless, in 1842 he ardently sought—and eventually received—an appointment to the finest engineering school in the nation: the U.S. Military Academy.

Jackson knew that he would have a difficult time mastering the curriculum at the academy, and he knew that West Point was the one chance he had to make something of his life. Painfully aware of his poor scholastic preparation, his physical awkwardness, and his lack of social graces, he nevertheless accepted the challenge. "You may be whatever you resolve to be" became the best known of several maxims he adopted while a cadet.

At West Point, he was so withdrawn that fellow cadets remembered him mostly with sympathy. A classmate described Jackson's years with this little-known but highly revealing summation:

> He was so modest and retiring in his ways as to be but little observed or known by other cadets. . . . In consequence of a somewhat shambling, awkward gait, and the habit of carrying his head down in a thoughtful attitude, he seemed less of stature than he really was. . . . An intense student, his mind appeared to be constantly preoccupied, and he seldom spoke to anyone unless spoken to, and then his face lighted up blushingly, as that of a bashful person when complimented. . . .
>
> His utterances were quick, jerky, and sententious, but when once made were there ended; there was no repetition or amending, no hypothesis or observation to lead to further discussion. When a jocular remark occurred in his hearing, he smiled as though he understood and enjoyed it, but never ventured comment to promote further mirth. . . .
>
> There were occasions, as I observed, when his actions appeared strangely affected; as, for instance, a drenching shower caught sections returning from recitations, or the battalion from the mess-hall, and ranks were broken to allow the cadets to rush for shelter to the barracks. Jackson would continue his march, solemnly, at the usual pace, deviating neither to the right or to the left. . . . He alone appeared to know [his plan], for no one bothered themselves to discover it or did more than to remark: "Look at Old Jackson!" . . . He was, as Ephraim was, "like unto a cake unturned," which, I presume, was only the biblical way of saying [Jackson] was a diamond in the rough.[18]

That diamond was not merely unbreakable; it shone in greater luster with each passing year at West Point. Through never-wavering diligence and persistence, the academic record of the orphan from the mountains steadily improved.[19] At Jackson's graduation in the famous class of 1846, he ranked seventeenth among fifty-nine cadets. Faculty and students alike insisted that if the curriculum had lasted another year, the shy and quiet Jackson would have ranked first.[20]

He quickly discovered that the military was his calling in life. From West Point, Jackson and other young officers proceeded to war in Mexico. His high standing enabled him to receive assignment to the artillery, his preferred branch of service. At Veracruz, Contreras, and Chapultepec the new lieutenant was conspicuous for fearlessness and devotion to duty. Jackson returned to the States a brevet major, the most decorated member of his West Point class.

Jackson learned many lessons in Mexico that served him well fourteen years later in the Civil War. He matriculated skillfully from textbook knowledge to practical application. Jackson recognized the importance of well-placed artillery, the advantage of flanking movements, the necessity for quick marches and heavy attacks at unexpected places. Further, Jackson saw and perfected the patience required in handling volunteer soldiers.

He utilized all of these skills in his dazzling movements and strikes in the 1862 valley campaign. Later that summer, a northern newspaper reporter traveled through the northern end of the region. After allegedly talking with several people who knew the "rebel Napoleon," the correspondent painted this picture of Jackson:

> As for the outer man, he looks at least seven years older than he is— his height is above five feet ten inches; his figure thick set, square shouldered, and decidedly clumsy; his gait very awkward, stooping, and with long strides. He often walks with his head somewhat on one side, and his eyes fixed upon the ground, imparting to his whole appearance that abstracted quality which young ladies describe as "absent-minded." A lady who has known him long and well, has told me that she never saw him on horseback without laughing— short stirrups, knees cramped up, heels stuck out behind, and chin on his breast—a most unmilitary phenomenon.[21]

Yes, Jackson differed from most people, and the impression has grown through the years that his virtues cannot be explained rationally: his genius in the field must have had mysterious, even miraculous, origins. Such is not the case. He was a rugged individualist, with emphasis on both words. These qualities contributed to his terrible reputation as a professor at the Virginia Military Institute, but other factors were involved as well. Fresh from the army, where discipline was paramount, Jackson demanded the same strict obedience from youthful cadets. Even though innately kind and polite, he enforced every rule with a rigidity many thought akin to rigor mortis. In the ten years he taught at the institute, Jackson was personally responsible for the expulsion of as many as a dozen cadets.

Ill health further hampered Jackson's classroom performance. Partial deafness in his right ear became a real impairment. Jackson worried as well about his throat, liver, kidneys, muscular network, and nervous system. At times he was convinced that every one of his major organs was malfunctioning. By a process of trial and error begun shortly after the Mexican War, Jackson concluded that the road to good health lay in hydropathy. Rarely a year passed in the decade thereafter when he did not spend extended periods at mineral springs and water-cure establishments from Virginia to Vermont.

To ease the pain of dyspepsia, he adopted an almost monastic diet that included no liquor, coffee, tea, butter, or fine foods. He rarely ate meat, and he refused to eat any dish of which he was deeply fond. At more than one dinner party, Jackson sat through the courses while declining to take anything but a glass of water. Even when the fare was simple enough for his digestion, Jackson never used pepper as seasoning. He once told an astonished hostess, "The moment a grain of pepper touches my tongue, I lose all strength in my right leg."[22] The one exception to not eating food he liked was fruit. Jackson loved every kind of fruit because he was certain of its beneficial qualities to his health. Besides, he liked the tastes. While peaches were his favorite "delicacy," he also enjoyed cherries, apples, watermelons, lemons, strawberries, and persimmons.

His vision began giving him problems after the Mexican War, probably an inflammation known as uveitis. To avoid taxing his weak sight, Jackson each afternoon would memorize the next day's lectures. In the evening he sat in a dark room and reviewed what he had committed to memory. The next morning he gave the presentation. This approach worked—unless a cadet asked for clarification on a certain point. Jackson was then helpless. All he could do was back up and recite verbatim the pertinent material he had memorized. Expanding upon a topic was simply beyond his ability. Moreover, if a cadet ventured to offer an answer not contained in either the lecture or the textbook, Jackson put the youth on report for insubordination. There was no place in his natural and experimental philosophy course for originality of thought. However, such is the case in many collegiate courses. Many of what were perceived as Jackson's oddities at the Virginia Military Institute resulted from first impressions, just as his overemphasized peculiarities in the Civil War emerged in the first year, not the second. College students progressing from the age of eighteen to the age of twenty-two undergo an astounding transformation in both thought and opinion. Freshmen saw Major Jackson as eccentric; first-classmen saw him as inspiring.

James T. Hubard was one of those cadets. In matriculating to upper-class status, he came to gain a full perspective on Jackson. Hubard commented that Jackson "knew perhaps as well as any man how to wear the dignity and reserve of a teacher, but when off duty he was always the familiar friend of his old pupils, and accessible to them all. He ranked high with all of us at the Institute, particularly for firmness and strength of character, and there was a universal feeling amongst us, that if 'Old Hickory'—as we called him—undertook to do anything, nothing under the sun could stop him."[23]

Younger cadets mocked him, played pranks on him, and ridiculed and criticized him, calling him "Tom Fool." One cadet dismissed Jackson as "a hell of a fool"; another thought him "crazy as damnation." Lines began circulating through the corps:

> The V. M. I., O what a spot
> In winter cold, in summer hot.
> Great Lord Al———, what a wonder
> Major Jackson, Hell & Thunder!

A thoroughly exasperated third-classman spoke for many when he exclaimed that Jackson was "undoubtedly the worst teacher that God ever made."[24]

As most of those youths matured into senior-class standing,

however, they understood the rudiments of leadership that Jackson strove so earnestly to impart to them. An overwhelming majority of cadets eventually developed a genuine admiration and deep respect for him. Students who regarded Jackson as a total curiosity matured into the Confederate captains, majors, and colonels who thought Jackson the most accomplished leader. And they followed him with an obedience that extended to a genuine willingness to risk their lives at his command.

The same first impressions prevailed among Lexington townspeople in the 1850s. Jackson surely seemed like an oddity in his first years in Shenandoah Valley society. Woe to anyone who, in Jackson's presence, sprinkled conversation with the phrase "you know." After each, Jackson would respond earnestly, "No, sir, I do not know."[25] At soirees he would seek out the young lady who struck him as the loneliest to keep her company. As a result, eligible women began to steer clear of Jackson at parties to avoid the stigma of being classed as the most unwanted of the guests.

He had peculiarities, to be sure. Yet within a decade, Jackson married twice into prominent families; he bought a home, acquired a farm, purchased stock in a local tannery, traveled widely, joined the Presbyterian Church, became a deacon, organized a young men's Bible class, taught a black Sunday school class, made political speeches before appreciative audiences, and served on the board of directors of the oldest bank in the county with a half-dozen of the community's most respected businessmen. Such accomplishments are not what one would expect from an odd and unpredictable individual. John T. L. Preston, one of Lexington's most influential residents at the time, put Jackson in clear perspective with this evaluation: "As a citizen and church member, he was the object of pleasant jests for singularities and peculiarities, but the confidence in his integrity, force of character, and soundness of mind was universal."[26]

One of Jackson's marriages brought him profound heartache, while the other generated happiness—but only for a little while. Jackson was twenty-nine when he fell in love for the first time. The object of his affection was Elinor Junkin, the daughter of a Presbyterian cleric who also was president of Washington College in Lexington. In August 1853, the couple wed. Fourteen months later, Ellie died in childbirth, as did the baby. Jackson was crushed by grief. He blurted out to an acquaintance, "Ah, if it only might please God to let me go now!" For several months he continued to wish for his own death.[27] A three-month summer tour of Europe in 1856 convinced Jackson that he must live and reap some of the benefits of earthly existence. He began a whirlwind courtship of another minister's daughter, Mary Anna Morrison. They married in the summer of 1857, but the joy of family was slow in coming. Their first child, a girl, lived only two weeks before dying of jaundice.

The loss of two children helps explain in some degree Jackson's affection for all children. Nothing secular in this world gave him greater pleasure than to frolic about a house with one or more "little people" on his back or laughing loudly around him. The man who was stern and relentless as a field commander became a veritable Santa Claus in the presence of children. Anna Jackson bore another child, a daughter born in 1862. She was five months old before Jackson saw her for the first time, and he died one month later.

Considerable misunderstanding surrounds Jackson's views on slavery. While at the Virginia Military Institute, he had two slaves, both of whom had asked him to purchase them, which he did with reluctance and Christian charity. Anna also owned a mammy and her two sons. Jackson's personal views on human bondage were typically simple. Slavery was something created by God for reasons man could not be expected to know. Since Jackson could not do anything about the institution (and he regarded it as sacrilege to consider any such action), he resolved to treat the black members of his family with fatherly attachment. He always insisted that his slaves absorb the tenets of the Christian faith. Toward that end, and initially alone, Jackson in 1855 began a Sunday school class for slaves of all ages in the Lexington area. A Virginia law specifically prohibited teaching slaves to read or write, so the major skirted the perimeter of legality in conducting the Sunday afternoon meetings. His undertaking was immediately successful. As many as one hundred slaves attended this school, and at every gathering the assemblage sang, "Amazing grace how sweet the sound / That saved a wretch like me." It was the only song Jackson knew. He was all but totally tone deaf. His affection for the slaves was genuine and shared. When Jackson learned during the war that his aged housekeeper, Amy, had died, he went to his tent and wept uncontrollably.

Although Jackson's personality, his creative tactical maneuvers, and his genius for arousing enthusiasm among his soldiers were not linked directly with each other, a common thread joined them and provided both orderliness and cohesion. That common thread, the third foundation for Jackson's charisma, was faith. For Jackson, religion was an overpowering, all-consuming devotion to God. A Virginia Military Institute graduate who served under Jackson in the Confederate army remarked, "To me he was my ideal of honorable, upright Christian manhood. God was in all his thoughts." One of Jackson's true friends, Colonel Frederick Holliday of the Thirty-third Virginia, recalled that with Jackson "the fierce thunderbolt of war was interwoven through and through with the tenderest Christian virtues." A brother-in-law, Confederate General D. H. Hill, commented in a private 1863 letter that "the striking characteristic" of Jackson's mind "was his profound reverence for divine and human authority. I never knew of any one whose reverence for Deity was so all pervading, and who felt so completely his entire dependence upon God."[28]

Many field commanders in American history have been God fearing; none has been as God loving as Jackson. A member of the Presbyterian congregation in Lexington declared, "It would be difficult to find in the entire Church any member who . . . found so much happiness in his religion." Jackson himself told Anna on more than one occasion, "I am cheered with an anticipated, glorious and luminous tomorrow. . . . No earthly calamity can shake my hope in the future so long as God is my friend."[29]

From the moment he pledged himself to God in 1851, Jackson regarded prayer as a necessity in life. He strove to be the personification of his favorite Bible verse, Romans 8:28: "And we know that all things work together for good to them that love God, to them that are called according to his purpose." The depth of Jackson's reliance on prayer can be seen in this observation: "I have so fixed the habit [of praying] in my own mind that I never raise a glass of water to my lips without a moment's asking of God's blessing. I never seal a letter without putting a word of prayer under the seal. I never take a letter from the post without a brief sending of my thoughts heavenward. I never change my classes in the section room without a minute's petition on the cadets who go out and those who come in."[30]

Jackson carried that complete devotion to God into the Civil War. As a Confederate general he honestly believed that he was doing the Lord's will. He prayed constantly that his command might become what he called "an army of the living God." His official reports contain such affirmations as "God blessed our arms with victory," "an ever-kind Providence blessed us with success," and "God has been our shield, and to His name be all the glory." After two weeks in the field in the spring of 1861, Jackson wrote to his wife from Harpers Ferry, "I am strengthening my position, & if attacked, shall with the blessing of that God, who has always been with me, & who I firmly believe will never forsake [me], repel the enemy."[31] In December 1862, Jackson informed his friend, General William E. "Grumble" Jones, that "through God's blessing the enemy suffered severely at [the battle of] Fredericksburg."[32] Jackson's usually stern and emotionless demeanor in battle gave way on another occasion to sublime joy. His men were driving to victory when the general turned to a staff officer and, with a radiant countenance, exulted, "He who does not see the hand of God in this is blind, sir, blind!"[33]

Jackson's faith assumed two different but profound forms. His statements did not contain references to Frederick the Great or Napoleon but to Joshua and King David. At the same time, Jackson loved God with the childlike cheerfulness of one who, like Saint Paul, had received an incomparable gift from above. For Jackson, battle was a blend of Old Testament fury and New Testament faith.

In camp or behind the lines, the childlike simplicity and soul-deep earnestness of Jackson's devotion to God impressed even his critics. If called upon to lead prayer at a religious service, he would rise, place his arms across his chest, raise his head, shut his eyes tightly, and implore divine blessing so intensely that his own dedication became infectious. On more than one occasion in combat, he lifted his arm and his eyes toward heaven and moved his lips as if in prayer. His soldiers would watch the motion with superstitious awe. Some later confessed that they felt as if God were leading them into the fight. Jackson was a soldier without fear. Early in the Civil War, a junior officer asked him how he kept so cool amid all the dangers of combat. Jackson responded quickly, "Captain, my religious belief teaches me to feel as safe in battle as in bed. God has fixed the time for my death. I do not concern myself about *that*, but always to be ready, no matter when it may overtake me."[34]

Being the foremost hero in the Confederacy fazed him little if at all. Jackson dismissed adoration from his mind. Late in 1862, he told his wife that "our ever gracious heavenly Father is exceedingly kind to me, and strikingly manifests it by the kindness with which he disposes people to treat me. . . . God, my exceeding great Joy, is continually showering His blessings upon me, an unworthy servant."[35]

But he also longed for peace. Before the sectional struggle was a year old, Jackson wrote, "I do hope that the war will soon be over, and that I shall never again have to take the field."[36] By the end of the second year of the war, Jackson dreamed of purchasing a tract somewhere in the Shenandoah Valley and spending the remainder of his life in the quietness of a gentleman farmer.[37]

His superb achievements on the battlefield ended disastrously at Chancellorsville. Wounded by friendly fire, Jackson underwent the amputation of an arm. The Confederate army waited anxiously, and Lee made no effort to hide his own concern. "Give him my affectionate regards," he told Jackson's chaplain, "and tell him to make haste and get well, and come back to me as soon as he can. He has lost his left arm, but I have lost my right arm."[38]

Hopes were futile. Complications arose from the wounds, and pneumonia developed. Jackson had always expressed a desire to die on the Lord's Day. Shortly after 3:00 P.M. on Sunday, May 10, 1863, he awakened briefly from unconsciousness. He smiled and said clearly, "Let us cross over the river, and rest under the shade of the trees."[39] Moments later, he was dead. Jackson's passing was the greatest personal loss suffered by the Confederacy. The largest crowd in the history of Richmond gathered to pay respects as the body lay in state in the capitol. Flags across Virginia and the South flew at half mast. Jackson was buried in Lexington, surrounded by the same mountains that nurtured him in his youth.

"I do not know how to replace him," a distraught Lee moaned at the news of his friend's death.[40] No replacement ever emerged. Perhaps it is too strong to say that the journey to Appomattox began on a Saturday night in May 1863, with an unfortunate volley of musketry in the darkness of the Virginia wilderness. However, a number of major conclusions can be reached about the course of Confederate fortunes in the field without Jackson.

After his death, Lee never again attempted the great offensive flank movement that Jackson five times executed with resounding success. Further, with Jackson vanished much of the daring, mobility, and aggressiveness that had brought victory after victory to the Army of Northern Virginia. On at least two occasions during the following year, a frustrated Lee criticized unsuccessful officers by asking why they did not do as Jackson would have done under similar circumstances. One of Jackson's veterans made a cogent postwar observation. In every defeat of Lee's army after Chancellorsville, he declared, the "foot cavalry" would exclaim, "Oh, if Jackson had been here, things would have been different!"[41]

These might-have-beens add much to Jackson's charisma, as did the timing of his death. He fell at the pinnacle of his career. He was never encumbered by the collapse of the Southern Confederacy; the missed opportunities at Gettysburg and elsewhere only added to the weight of his loss. Just as speculation occurs about how the reunion of North and South after the Civil War might have differed had Abraham Lincoln's soft but firm touch been present, so is there endless conjecture over the course of the war had Jackson remained at Lee's side.

Jackson's innate ability to lead with extraordinary power, to command respect, loyalty, and love from his men, to have no other gods before him but that of the Creator, to be void of such human weaknesses as vanity and ambition, combined with his tragic death at a critical moment in the war, have elevated him to legendary stature if not to immortal status. One hopes that designating Jackson "a pious, blue-eyed killer" was the result of ignorance and not of malice.

If one combines Webster's two definitions into one, *charisma* becomes "a divinely inspired gift that captures the popular imagination and inspires allegiance and devotion." The result is a perfect description of General Stonewall Jackson. He could accept this statement, yet two things would have pleased him more. A hymn written by Sabine Boring-Gould only a year after Jackson's death would have become the general's favorite because of its stirring chorus: "Onward, Christian soldiers, marching as to war / With the cross of Jesus going on before." Far greater contentment would have come to Jackson in knowing that his reunited country has prospered and still lives under a simple motto that embodies his whole life: "In God We Trust."

Notes

1. Unidentified Dallas newspaper clipping, in possession of the author.

2. H. Kyd Douglas of Jackson's staff called the general "the most awkward horseman I ever saw." A newspaperman who watched Jackson in action at Fredericksburg thought him "the most ungraceful rider in the army—and who naturally sways from side to side as if he were 'three sheets in the wind.'" To an officer and graduate of the Virginia Military Institute, Jackson was not an impressive rider except "when the soldiers were cheering him; then he would straighten himself in the saddle, and ride erect, with uncovered head and at a rapid pace, as if to escape this ovation of his troops." Marginal note by Douglas in his copy of G. F. R. Henderson, *Stonewall Jackson and the American Civil War* (London and New York: Longmans, Green, 1898), 1:22, Douglas Library, Antietam National Battlefield Park, Maryland; *Staunton Spectator,* December 30, 1862; George M. Vickers, ed., *Under Both Flags* (St. Louis, Mo.: People's Publishing, 1896), 135.

3. Mary Anna Jackson, *Memoirs of Stonewall Jackson* (Louisville, Ky.: Prentice Press, 1895), 287.

4. *Saturday Evening Post,* December 1914, quoted in Thomas J. Arnold, *Early Life and Letters of General Thomas J. Jackson* (New York: Fleming H. Revell, 1916), 344.

5. William S. White, *Sketches of the Life of Captain Hugh A. White, of the Stonewall Brigade* (Columbia: South Carolinian Steam Press, 1864), 99.

6. John H. Worsham, *One of Jackson's Foot Cavalry* (Jackson, Tenn.: McCowat-Mercer Press, 1964), 102–3.

7. *Richmond Daily Dispatch*, February 10, 1863.

8. David French Boyd, *Reminiscences of the War in Virginia* (Austin, Tex.: Jenkins Publishing Company, 1989), 7.

9. For Jackson's plain appearance, see Allen C. Redwood, "With Stonewall Jackson," *Scribner's Magazine* 18 (1879): 223; *Confederate Veteran* 30 (1922): 61; Jennings C. Wise, *The Military History of the Virginia Military Institute from 1839 to 1865* (Lynchburg, Va.: J. P. Bell, 1915), 159–60.

10. *Century Magazine* 47 (1893–94): 627–28. See also Henry Kyd Douglas, *I Rode with Stonewall* (Chapel Hill: University of North Carolina Press, 1940), 17, 35.

11. M. Graham Ellzey to James H. Lane, December 1, 1888, Lane Papers, Auburn University, Auburn, Ala.

12. Robert U. Johnson and C. C. Buel, eds., *Battles and Leaders of the Civil War* (New York: Century Company, 1884–88), 2:297. A slightly different version of Jackson's statement appears in Jedediah Hotchkiss to William L. Chase, March 28, 1892, Jedediah Hotchkiss Papers, reel 39, Library of Congress (hereafter abbreviated as LC).

13. *Confederate Veteran* 9 (1901): 379.

14. Charles W. Squires, "Autobiography," LC.

15. James H. Lane Reminiscences, Lane Papers, Auburn University; Jackson, *Memoirs*, 564.

16. Richard Taylor, *Destruction and Reconstruction: Personal Experiences of the Late War* (New York: D. Appleton and Company, 1879), 49–50, 80.

17. Percy Gatling Hamlin, *"Old Bald Head" (General R. S. Ewell)* (Strasburg, Va.: Shenandoah, 1940), 104–5.

18. John Caldwell Tidball Reminiscences, U.S. Military Academy, West Point, N.Y.

19. Jackson achieved extraordinarily good marks in behavior at West Point. In his junior year at the academy, he led the corps of cadets, receiving no demerits.

20 For example, see Dabney H. Maury, *Recollections of a Virginian in the Mexican, Indian, and Civil Wars* (New York: C. Scribner's Sons, 1894), 23.

21. Undated newspaper clipping, S. Joseph Bershtein Collection, Clarksburg, W.Va., Public Library.

22. Raleigh Edward Colston Reminiscences, Southern Historical Collection, University of North Carolina, Chapel Hill (hereafter cited as SHC).

23. James T. Hubard to Robert L. Dabney, September 17, 1863, Charles W. Dabney Papers, box 19, SHC.

24. Thomas B. Robinson textbook, Virginia Military Institute; Charles M. Barton to Joseph M. Barton, September 28, 1855, Barton Collection, SHC. See also *Southern Historical Society Papers* 16 (1888): 44–45; 20 (1892): 308–9.

25. William C. Chase, *Story of Stonewall Jackson* (Atlanta: D. E. Luther, 1901), 159; *Century Magazine* 32 (1886): 929.

26. John T. L. Preston Narrative, Dabney Papers, box 20, SHC.

27. Elizabeth Preston Allan, *The Life and Letters of Margaret Junkin Preston* (Boston and New York: Houghton, Mifflin and Company, 1903), 77.

28. Thomas W. Baldwin Reminiscences, in possession of the writer; Jackson, *Memoirs*, 624; Daniel Harvey Hill to Robert L. Dabney, June 7, 1863, Robert Lewis Dabney Papers, Union Theological Seminary, New York.

29. William A. Anderson, *Address of William A. Anderson, upon the Laying of the Corner-Stone of the Equestrian Statue to Stonewall Jackson: In Richmond, Virginia, on June 3, 1915, at the Request of the Stonewall Jackson Monument Corporation* (Richmond, Va.: n.p., 1915?), 5. See also May 24, 1863, sermon, George William White Collection, Presbyterian Church (U.S.A.) Archives, Montreat, N.C. For Jackson's expressions of faith to his wife, see Jackson, *Memoirs*, 247, 254, 283, 297, 312, 327.

30. *Century Magazine* 32 (1886): 935.

31. Thomas J. Jackson to Anna Jackson, May 8, 1861, Thomas Jonathan Jackson Papers, Library of Virginia, Richmond.

32. Thomas J. Jackson to William E. Jones, December 1862, E. A. Burke Collection, Louisiana State University, Baton Rouge.

33. *Southern Historical Society Papers* 25 (1897): 107. A different, popular, but hearsay version of Jackson's exclamation appears in Robert L. Dabney, *Life and Campaigns of Lieut.-Gen. Thomas J. Jackson (Stonewall Jackson)* (Richmond, Va.: National Publishing, 1866), 531.

34. Johnson and Buel, eds., *Battles and Leaders*, 1:238.

35. Thomas J. Jackson to Anna Jackson, November 11, 1862, Robert L. Dabney Papers, Library of Virginia.

36. Jackson, *Memoirs*, 249.

37 Ibid., 204.

38. Beverly Tucker Lacy Narrative, Dabney Papers, box 20, SHC.

39 Jackson, *Memoirs*, 457.

40. J. William Jones, *Life and Letters of Robert Edward Lee: Soldier and Man* (New York: Neale Publishing, 1906), 242.

41. In a conversation with Colonel William Allan only eight months before Lee died, the general confessed that he often thought how the battle of Gettysburg would have ended differently had Jackson been there (Allan, "Conversations with Lee," William Allan Papers, vol. 3, SHC). See also Lane Reminiscences, Auburn University; Launcelot M. Blackford, *Mine Eyes Have Seen the Glory: The Story of a Virginia Lady, Mary Berkeley Minor Blackford, 1802–1896, Who Taught Her Sons to Hate Slavery and to Love the Union* (Cambridge: Harvard University Press, 1954), 221; *Confederate Veteran* 21 (1913): 494.

Jubal Anderson Early in 1869, shortly after his return to the United States from Canada. Courtesy Library of Congress.

From Antebellum Unionist
to Lost Cause Warrior:
The Personal Journey
of Jubal A. Early

Gary W. Gallagher

JUBAL ANDERSON EARLY took the floor to address the Virginia State Convention on April 16, 1861. Abraham Lincoln's call for 75,000 militia to suppress the Lower South's rebellion had spurred enthusiasm for secession, which Early hoped to dampen. "I have sat in my seat all day, and imagined that I could see a ball of flame hanging over this body," Early told his fellow delegates, adding that secession would be "a great crime . . . against the cause of liberty and civilization." He insisted that support for the Union was "in the interest of my country, in the interest of my State, and in the interest of the cause of liberty itself." He warned that departing the Union would bring "such a war as this country has never seen." Although the convention voted for secession the next day, Early did not. Six years later he expressed radically different sentiments while watching events in the United States from self-imposed exile in Canada. An important Confederate officer during the Civil War, Early had gone abroad to escape what he termed "Yankee rule" by Republican politicians whom he labeled "infernal demons who sit at Washington in unrestrained power." "I would like to begin the fight over right now," he stated, "though with the certainty that we would be exterminated. I have got to that condition, that I think I could scalp a Yankee woman and child without winking my eyes."[1]

Early's quick conversion to support for the Confederacy and his unreconstructed postwar hostility toward the North seemingly stand at odds with his unionist stance in 1861. Yet the temptation to assume a major shift in Early's thinking overlooks a bedrock continuity concerning political and social questions. The key to understanding him lies in his self-styled "conservatism." Amid sea changes shaped by the sectional struggle over slavery, four years of civil war, and more than a decade of Reconstruction, Early remained steadfastly devoted to the same basic principles. He embraced an antebellum world ordered by a constitution that protected property, a hierarchical social structure dominated by members of the slaveholding elite, and rigid racial conventions that guaranteed white supremacy. He consistently resisted changes in this world, functioned comfortably when part of a political minority within Virginia (which was most of the time), and, although often involved with politics and public issues, never trimmed his sails to satisfy public opinion. At the same time, he believed it every citizen's duty to yield what he called a "patriotic submission" to any government that remained true to the Constitution—even if the government was controlled by the opposing party. Early's willingness to stand apart from the mainstream extended to his private life, where he flouted social conventions accepted by the vast majority of his contemporaries. True to himself, he accepted the consequences: "I was never what is called a popular man," he bluntly conceded in his memoirs.[2]

Some historians have read into Early's role as a prominent Lost Cause warrior a desire to rationalize his support for the Confederacy and to obscure his military failures during the Civil War. Perhaps most influential has been Thomas L. Connelly's work, which portrays a marginal man—"one of [Robert E.] Lee's most disliked subordinates" who fashioned a record during the war that "held no promise of postwar eminence." Following Early's unsuccessful campaign in the Shenandoah Valley in 1864, notes Connelly, "Violent protests by some Virginians in the area compelled Lee to remove him from command." Early subsequently settled in Canada, whence he explained to those left behind that "he had chosen exile rather than submit 'to the yoke of the oppressors,' and begged ex-Rebels to understand the reasons why he had abandoned them." For a man who first opposed secession, then fought for it, and finally fled the South while other ex-Confederates remained, argues Connelly, "Early protested too much. . . . He always overreacted, blaming his hatred of the North for his decision." Between the lines of Early's letters from Canada lies "the guilt of one who obviously felt he had deserted the South in a period of crisis."[3]

Connelly maintains that by taking the lead in Lost Cause efforts to vindicate the Confederacy and canonize Lee, Early cloaked himself in his hero's mantle of greatness. Protection of Lee's military reputation against all questioners actually betrayed a deeper wish. "[T]he ferocity of Early's rebuttals masked a significant reason for his self-assumed role" as Lee's protector: "Though many cowered from his pen, it was perhaps Early who was more afraid. Early's own record was replete with errors which he tried to conceal by attacking others' reputations." Connelly pronounces Early a "stereotype of the basic paradoxical nature of the southern mind." He fought secession in 1861 but when Virginia left the Union "became the most rebellious of all Rebels—a crude, profane 'Yankee-hating' individual."[4]

The best biography of Early accepts Connelly's interpretive framework for the postwar years. In *Jubal*, Charles C. Osborne sketches a man incapable of accepting "history's chastisement" of southern white people who hoped through Lost Cause propagandistic efforts "to handle the psychological trauma of defeat." Unlike Lee and most other former Confederates, Early refused to acknowledge the reality "that Northern victory had altered the landscape of their lives," making no attempt "to live according to the new topography." Given Early's "vehement and articulate irreconcilability," he naturally emerged as a leading Lost Cause voice and heavily influenced late-nineteenth-century writings about the war. "In wielding that influence," states Osborne, "Early and his adherents had the satisfaction of achieving a recognition they had never known during the Civil War."

Gaines M. Foster's elegant *Ghosts of the Confederacy* places Early among a group of former Confederates who "brooded over defeat, railed against the North, and offered the image of the Confederacy as an antidote to change." While not closely tied to the planter class, suggests Foster, these men had been part of the prewar southern and Confederate elites. They offered a historical vision that "promoted older aristocratic values" and urged southern white people to "return to the ways of a better time." Increasingly out of touch with the postwar reality, they "appeared captivated by a dream of victory, a dream of a return to an undefeated Confederacy." Overwhelming Northern numbers and James Longstreet's perfidy at Gettysburg and elsewhere had brought down Lee and the Confederacy, asserted Early and his cohorts, as they endlessly examined the military history of the war in search of factors that enabled the brutish North to triumph over the more admirable Confederacy. In a marvelous image that casts Early as a hopeless outsider, Foster compares him and his supporters to the ghost dancers who emerged among the Plains Indians at about the same time: "One can easily imagine a gathering of Early and company, wearing their gray ghost shirts. . . . Formed in a circle about a statue of a recumbent Lee, the true believers dance in and back, chanting, on one foot, 'overwhelming numbers,' and on the other, 'betrayed by Longstreet'—waiting for an undefeated, marble Lee to rise and lead them to victory."[5]

Despite their many insights, these writers miss the point that Early's response to changes wrought by the war merely continued an antebellum pattern of resisting anything that threatened his conservative worldview. Northern actions during the conflict—especially emancipation and what Early viewed as outrages against Confederate civilians and their property—certainly affected him, but a strong thread of consistency runs through his entire life. Moreover, a tendency in recent scholarship to remove Early from the mainstream of southern life before and after the war diminishes his actual role. For the better part of five decades he maintained a vigorous correspondence with politicians, sought to influence political events at various levels (often successfully), and attained substantial stature as a local and state figure. During the war, his contributions placed him immediately behind Stonewall Jackson and Longstreet among Lee's corps commanders. Although his unswerving political conservatism placed him at odds with the majority of Virginians both before and after the war, Early nonetheless remained a figure to be reckoned with until the mid-1880s.

Young Early's personal philosophy took shape within a family related to some of the wealthiest planters in the South. He was born on November 3, 1816, in Franklin County, Virginia, the third child and second son of Joab and Ruth Hairston Early. Relatives on both sides of the family stood solidly among the slaveholding elite. At one time Joab Early's holdings included more than 1,000 acres of land in Franklin County, and from the 1830s through the end of the antebellum era he owned several dozen slaves. Ruth Early's extended family included an uncle, Samuel Hairston of Pittsylvania County, who in the mid-1850s owned several plantations and more than 1,500 slaves. Joab Early served his county as a colonel of militia and one-term member of the Virginia House of Delegates, and he imparted to his son a strong allegiance to the Whig Party. Jubal thus spent his formative years in a household of abundant material goods, where respect for property stood high and the Democratic Party's increasing celebration of the common man found scant approval.[6]

Early's reaction to events in Texas and Mexico during the 1830s and 1840s foreshadowed his response to the outbreak of war in 1861. While still a cadet at West Point, he expressed a passionate desire to enlist in the Texas revolution against Mexico. The Mexican people had adopted in 1824 a national constitution "modelled after ours," he observed, with a "*General Government,* and also several state Governments, each of which was as independent as our State Governments are." Americans living in the Mexican state of Texas had taken up their new residences in good faith, but within "the last year or so, Santa Anna, aided by the Priests and the Military, has usurped the

Government, overturned the constitution, and established an almost unbounded despotism over what was once the free states of Mexico." Santa Anna had violated the compact implicit between the central government and the American immigrants and sought "to deprive Texas of its free constitution." In language similar to that he would employ twenty-five years later concerning Lincoln's actions as president, Early concluded that Texans "resisting the Tyranny and barbarous cruelty of an *usurped* government" deserved the sympathy and support of anyone who believed in liberty and the rule of constitutional authority.

Early remained at West Point rather than joining the Texans, subsequently dividing his antebellum energies among military, legal, and political endeavors. He graduated from the academy in 1837 and served against the Seminoles in Florida before resigning in July 1838 to pursue a career in the law. An attorney in Franklin County when tensions mounted between the United States and Mexico, he supported the Whig Party's popular standard-bearer, Senator Henry Clay of Kentucky. "Though I had voted, in the presidential election of 1844, for Mr. Clay, who opposed the annexation of Texas," Early wrote in his memoirs, "when war ensued, I felt it to be my duty to sustain the government in that war and to enter the military service if a fitting opportunity offered." The call for a regiment of federal volunteers from Virginia afforded such an opportunity, and Early accepted a commission as major of the First Regiment of Virginia Volunteers. Although he saw no combat during the war, he often commanded the regiment, and his position as one of its three field-grade officers earned him a statewide reputation. For the remainder of his antebellum career, Virginians referred to him as Major Early. A dozen years of practicing law in Rocky Mount—the seat of Franklin County—after the war with Mexico brought Early to the eve of the secession crisis.[7]

During the antebellum period Early never abandoned the Whig Party, whose members he frequently called conservatives. Elected as a Whig to the Virginia legislature for the 1841–42 term, he lost his bid for reelection by a wide margin to Democrat N. M. Taliaferro (under whom he had read law). A decade as commonwealth's attorney in Franklin and Floyd Counties followed his defeat in 1843. He mounted another bid for the state legislature in 1853, suffered a stinging rebuke from the voters, then watched sadly as the Whig Party shriveled in much of the South. At a meeting in Rocky Mount in 1856, he offered resolutions designed to help resuscitate Virginia's Whig Party, "to which it is our pride to belong, and in whose principles and conservative patriotism we have an abiding and undiminished confidence." Between 1840 and 1852, Early voted Whig in presidential canvasses and in 1856 supported Millard Fillmore as a fusion candidate of the Know-Nothings and the Whigs. As late as February 1860, long after organized opposition to the Democratic Party had collapsed across most of the South, Early addressed a gathering in Franklin County about the merits of holding a state convention of Whigs and Know-Nothings to mount a challenge to the Democrats. Upon Early's death in 1894, the *Lynchburg News* characterized him as "a life-long Whig, of the most conservative type."[8]

What did Early mean when he described himself as a conservative Whig? A good indication may be found in a July 1850 statement addressed to the voters of Franklin, Henry, and Patrick Counties in which he stressed the importance of property, respect for the Constitution, and the dangers of mob rule. Standing for a position as delegate to a state convention called to amend Virginia's constitution, Early pointed to "unmistakable signs of an approaching conflict, between the conservative principles of all true government on the one hand, and the turbulent and disecrating spirit of innovation on the other." He alluded to demands from western Virginia, home to a majority of the state's white people, to establish representation on the basis of white population, remove property qualifications for voters, and otherwise shift power away from slaveholders. Early asserted that the present constitution afforded "ample protection for our persons and property" but accepted the need for managed change to ward off more revolutionary tampering with the system. Delegates to the convention, he hoped, would neither "discard the admonitions and teachings of the wise fathers of the republic" nor "disregard the experience of the last seventy-five years." He warned that "every innovation is not reform—every change is not improvement."

Early grudgingly backed extending the franchise to all white males over twenty-one years of age but insisted on calling the vote a privilege rather than a right. He would not concede that representation should be based on white population alone, urging a formula derived from white population and assessed value that would favor slaveholders. Communities with equal populations but different amounts of property "should be entitled to different degrees of political importance, in a just ratio compounded of population and property." Government had been created to make property safe, he stated, "and nine tenths of the laws enacted are intended for the security and protection of property." People had acquiesced in the formation of governments that took a portion of the populace's natural rights in return for safeguarding "the enjoyment of what they had acquired, or might acquire, as the labor of their hands or the result of their skill." On the basis of this "great conservative principle," he admonished voters, "Take away this security and you destroy the main consideration of the [governmental] compact, render property insecure and the whole fabric of society will tumble in ruins."[9]

The election of delegates revealed a firm consensus opposed to Early's views. Listed as a "conservative" in the *Lynchburg Virginian*'s tally of the returns, he finished ninth among ten candidates with just 202 of nearly 7,000 votes cast. He subsequently characterized the election as an instance where "the people seemed to run wild in favor" of "radical changes, miscalled reforms."[10] Early clearly feared that white people of inferior social and economic station could disrupt an existing system that protected the hegemony and property of slaveholders.

Early supported the Union because its Constitution had enabled propertied white southerners to prosper. Unlike growing numbers of his southern contemporaries, he opposed extreme positions on issues related to slavery. Amid the vituperative debates over the legislation that would form the Compromise of 1850, he expressed a wish that "the efforts of the disunionists in both Quarters of the country to produce trouble, may be unavailing." He initially endorsed President Zachary Taylor's efforts to quiet the shrill debate over whether California should be a free state and the New Mexico territory organized on the basis of popular sovereignty; however, when it seemed the slaveholding Taylor conceded too much to the Free Soilers, Early backed away from him. Similarly, Early explained that "conservative men" rejected popular sovereignty as a solution to the Kansas-Nebraska turmoil of the mid-1850s because it could revive "the fires of the former agitation" regarding slavery in the territories.[11]

Early hoped divisions related to slavery would give way before a common resolve to honor the Constitution, which explicitly protected slave property and, excepting the foreign slave trade and the guarantee for the return of fugitive slaves, "left its regulation in every particular, where it belonged, that is to the several states where it existed." If northern states that had abolished slavery did not wish to be allied with those that retained it, they should have voted against ratification of the Constitution. "Having ratified it," concluded Early in a long postwar essay, "the faith of those states became pledged by every consideration that can bind states as communities, or men as individuals, to respect the institutions, rights and property of the other states and to faithfully abide by all of the compromises and guarantees of the Constitution." Millard Fillmore's "prudent, wise and national course"—especially his support of the Compromise of 1850 in the face of strong opposition from radical proslavery and antislavery forces—justified Whig support in 1856.[12]

For conservatives such as Early, no antebellum event more starkly underscored the absence of respect for the Constitution than the northern response to John Brown's raid on Harpers Ferry in October 1859. Speaking to a large crowd in Rocky Mount on December 5, 1859, Major Early explained why adherents of all political parties had been summoned to meet. Brown's "wicked and diabolical" actions threatened "to inaugurate a servile insurrection . . . for the purpose of destroying by force the institution of domestic slavery as it exists among us." Many northerners approved of Brown's raid, Early averred, and far too few had spoken forcefully against it. As a domestic institution, slavery should not be subject to interference from the North in the form of "moral suasion, legislative enactment, or physical force." Yet here was an example of northern citizens who chose to ignore the guarantees of the Constitution—leaving "the citizens of the South . . . [to] do all in their power to resist such interference."[13]

Brown's raid had threatened an institution Early believed fundamental to maintaining an ordered society in the South. Although federal census returns and local tax lists indicate that he probably never owned more than one slave himself (which meant his personal economic stake in slavery was marginal), Early worried about the sanctity of property in general and about the security of his family's extensive slave holdings in particular.[14] Perhaps equally important, he considered slavery the best means of controlling several million African Americans who lived in the antebellum South. By the late eighteenth century, he wrote in *The Heritage of the South*, abolition would have menaced white society and the American economy. "[T]he slaves bore such a proportion to the white population and the whole business of the country was so identified with their labor," he argued, "that it was impossible to emancipate them, without entailing on both races evils far greater than those supposed to result from the existence of slavery itself." The founding generation recognized this, shielded slave property in the Constitution, and wisely chose not to embrace what Early called "the dangerous experiment of the ideal schemes of a false philanthropy."[15]

Early joined most white southerners (and northerners) in believing that the Creator had stamped black people "with a different colour and an inferior physical and mental organization." Any mixing of the races would contravene the Lord's design, he thought, and slavery, which had advanced the descendants of "degraded Africans" to a "civilized and christianized condition," represented the best arrangement for all concerned. A passage in the preface to Early's 1866 memoir encapsulates his thinking on the subject: "Reason, common sense, true humanity to the black, as well as the safety of the white race, required that the inferior race should be kept in a state of subordination."[16]

The antebellum era closed in Virginia with its citizens watching the convention that convened in Richmond on February 13, 1861, to consider secession. Among the convention's unionist majority was Early, who, along with another former Whig, easily won election from Franklin County. The *Lynchburg Virginian,* which described Early as for the "Union straight out," greeted the Franklin County returns with wonder: "Eleven hundred majority for the Conservative ticket. Who would have thought it?" Democrats as well as former Whigs had supported Early as a moderate voice in a time of hot passions. Washington Dickinson, an erstwhile political foe, conceded past differences but told the major it was a time for "conservative men like yourself to come to the rescue, and save the sinking ship." This man admired Early's "consistency and conservatism" and hoped he would take the field against disunion, put party aside, and refrain from leveling blame against any faction. If men such as Early failed, Dickinson predicted darkly, doom would come in the form of civil war.[17]

Virginia unionists found few greater champions at the convention than Early. Secession represented to him an unjustifiable break with the Constitution that might affect the stability of slavery and society, and he repeatedly extolled the virtues of the existing system. Sometimes he stressed economics, as when he predicted that the loss of northern markets would hurt Virginia's tobacco industry (a key segment of the economy in his part of the state). Most often he urged fellow delegates to see the wisdom of remaining under the benevolent protection of the Constitution. On March 6, for example, he stated that Lincoln's promise to execute federal laws in all the states should "have been hailed throughout the country as a guarantee that he would perform his duty, and that we should have peace and protection for our property, and that the fugitive slave law would be faithfully executed." What of the secessionist claim that only departing the Union would protect the white South's minority rights? "I have been in a minority all my life," Early remarked in reference to his membership in the Whig Party, and "I have been standing up against currents that few men of my humble capacity could with-

stand, in defence of the rights of the minority." But secession represented the wrong method of preserving the rights of the southern
minority. "[C]an these rights be asserted, not by force or violence,
but under the Constitution and according to the laws?" he asked rhe-
torically. "I think they can, sir."[18]

When many delegates cheered the Confederate decision to fire
on Fort Sumter, Early countered that the act had placed a gulf between the seceded states and Virginia. He prophesied that a Confederate army might attempt to march through the commonwealth
toward Washington, expressing a desire that any such aggressive
action would arouse Virginia's sons to resist the Confederacy. Upon
passage of the state's ordinance of secession on April 17, Early pro-
nounced himself "perfectly satisfied . . . that a conflict will take place
between our citizens and the authorities of the General Government."
He made no apology for his vote against secession, regretting only
that he had swayed so few of his colleagues.

Yet once the die was cast only a single option remained—support for Virginia. Just as he had opposed war with Mexico and then
volunteered to serve, he also immediately acknowledged a duty to
sustain his state in this new crisis. He would yield his "patriotic submission" to its authorities and thereby make good on his promise
voiced in the convention on April 6: "I trust in God, that when
Virginia's hour of trial does come, I will have the nerve and the ability to do my duty. . . . My fortunes are with her, and shall ever be
with her, under all circumstances, through weal or woe. I shall neither desert her in her hour of prosperity, her hour of adversity, her
hour of glory, or her hour of shame. She is my mother, and I will
stand by her under all circumstances."[19]

Virginia's secession prompted Early to train his conservative lens
on a new array of problems. He believed an imminent confrontation
with the United States required that Virginia take defensive measures. On the day of the vote for secession, he said it was "absolutely
necessary to have a force in the field under the control of the State
authorities." Moreover, he thought authorizing the governor to sum-
mon the state's "military forces into the field is a conservative mea-

sure." Property and liberty headed the list of what Early sought to conserve through mobilization. Lincoln might send Federal troops through the state to reach the Deep South, or, worse yet, employ them against Virginia. Part of Early's own family lay at special risk because they had moved from Franklin County to the western fringe of the state. "I have an aged father living within thirteen miles of the Ohio, with some thirty or forty negroes," he observed on April 26. Joab Early's location "in the most exposed portion of that region" rendered his slaves and other property vulnerable to Federal incursions across the Ohio River.[20]

For two weeks after the vote on secession Early labored on the convention's military affairs committee. He recommended Robert E. Lee and Joseph E. Johnston as men capable of commanding armies, urged the state to call for volunteers rather than rely on its militia, and, showing a flash of his sarcastic and self-deprecating humor, claimed that the "necessities of the State require that all the Generals of Militia should be decapitated" and offered his "own head on the block as a willing victim for the good of the Commonwealth." As one of the state's prominent Mexican War veterans, Early attracted attention as a potential commander. "We are all looking to you as our leader," wrote a friend from Rocky Mount in late April. "[W]e all see that you are preparing to defend Va." In a letter to Governor John Letcher dated May 2, 1861, Early expressed his desire "to contribute as far as I can to the defense of the State if it shall be invaded."[21]

Fifteen days had taken Early from unqualified support for the Union to potential military service against the government of the United States. Willingness to oppose the old flag followed naturally from his antebellum beliefs. He had pursued a unionist course until the convention voted for secession, submitting to the will of the state's majority only after making his best arguments against separation. When Lincoln's actions in late April violated Early's conception of the constitutional compact between the United States and Virginia—to which he always had turned for protection of property and civil order—he felt duty bound to stand by his state.

He signed the ordinance of secession in late May (after Virginia's voters had ratified it), taking the opportunity to explain his reasons. Lincoln's aggressive policies against the South had "set aside the Constitution and laws and subverted the government of the United States," he claimed in language that recalled his 1835 letter concerning Texas. The Republican president headed a usurped government founded "on the worst principles of tyranny," and Early affixed his signature to the ordinance "with the intention of sustaining the liberties, independence and entity of the State of Virginia." He continued to hope, however, for "a reconstruction of the old Union in any manner that shall unite the people of Virginia with the people of the non-slave states of the North." Five years later Early recalled that adoption of the ordinance "wrung from me bitter tears of grief." "Any scruples which I may have entertained as to the right of secession," he added, "were soon dispelled by the mad, wicked, and unconstitutional measures of the authorities in Washington, and the frenzied clamour of the people of the North for war upon their former brethren of the South."[22]

Four years of fighting deepened Early's bitterness toward the northern government and people. In Virginia and across the rest of the former Confederacy, emancipation swept away billions of dollars in property and raised the specter of African-American challenges to white supremacy. Federal armies rendered desolate large areas of northern Virginia, the lower Shenandoah Valley, and other parts of the commonwealth. Joab Early joined thousands of other refugees who lost homes and significant property. Jubal Early himself wandered toward the Mississippi River as fighting ceased, eventually leaving the country via Mexico and settling in Toronto after brief stops in Havana and elsewhere. His military reputation, established in the eyes of fellow Virginians during the Mexican War and burnished by excellent service from First Manassas through the 1864 Overland Campaign, lay in tatters as a result of his decisive defeats at the hands of Philip H. Sheridan in the Shenandoah Valley. A woman in Charlottesville who saw Early shortly after his final debacle at Waynesboro in March 1865 voiced a common sentiment in her diary: "Oh! how are the mighty fallen! Gen. Early came in this evening with six men, having been hid somewhere in the mountains. He used to be a very great man." Writing two days earlier, an artillerist in Richmond had employed more scathing language in noting a report that Early had been captured: "What a pity they did not get him six (6) months ago. It would have been a lucky thing for the country."[23]

After his return from Canada in 1869, Early played a major role in the Lost Cause movement and took an active interest in conservative Democratic politics. A lucrative connection with the Louisiana lottery from the mid-1870s until his death afforded a comfortable living, freeing him to write and lecture extensively. As president of the Southern Historical Society and of the Association of the Army of Northern Virginia, frequent speaker, and indefatigable controversialist, he celebrated Lee's military accomplishments and praised the virtues of the whiggish slaveholding civilization he had lauded before the conflict. He also published a reminiscence defending his campaign in the Shenandoah Valley, wherein he emphasized Sheridan's overwhelming advantages in numbers and materiel. Almost everything he said and wrote conveyed a sense of bitterness toward the North while reaffirming his antebellum political and ideological views. On questions related to slavery, race, and politics, the postwar Early scarcely deviated from the prewar model. He also retained a characteristic willingness to stand apart from the majority if he thought principle demanded it.

Early's anger toward the North stemmed from what he considered assaults against the sanctity of property and the stable social order of the antebellum years. He viewed as outrageous Federal military transgressions against Confederate civilians and their property. During the Mexican War, Early had gained experience with an enemy's civilian population when he served for a time as military governor of Monterrey. He prided himself on the fact that he established excellent relations with the Mexicans under his control. According to Early, some of the residents of Monterrey told him he was the best governor they ever had. "It was generally conceded by officers of the army and Mexicans," he asserted, "that better order reigned in the city during the time I commanded there, than had ever before existed, and the good conduct of my men won for them universal praise."[24]

Federal armies during the Civil War exhibited behavior that differed markedly from this model of restrained, fair treatment of an enemy's population and their property. Early's memoir of the last year of the war, which he completed before the end of 1865, condemned the destructive activities of soldiers commanded by David Hunter and Sheridan in the Shenandoah Valley. In the wake of Hunter's army, "Houses had been burned, and helpless women and children left without shelter. The country had been stripped of provisions and many families left without a morsel to eat. Furniture and bedding had been cut to pieces, and old men and women and children robbed of all the clothing they had except that on their backs." Early labeled such depredations "wanton, cruel, unjustifiable, and cowardly" and refused to "insult the memory of the ancient barbarians . . . by calling them 'acts of Vandalism.'" Elsewhere, he pointed to the burning of Darien, Georgia, in 1863, and of Atlanta in 1864 by William Tecumseh Sherman as further evidence of Federal viciousness. In his persistent criticism of the North's military and political leaders, Early directed his strongest invective against those associated with the harshest policies toward civilians and their belongings—among them Grant, Sherman, Hunter, John Pope (whose appearance in Virginia in the summer of 1862 had marked a turning point toward harsher war), and the prominent Radical Republican Thaddeus Stevens.[25]

Federal abuses so angered Early that he ordered northern civilian property to be burned on a pair of well-known occasions. During the Confederate march through Pennsylvania in June 1863, his soldiers destroyed an ironworks owned by Thaddeus Stevens, and the following summer cavalrymen attached to his command put Chambersburg, Pennsylvania, to the torch. Taking full responsibility for both actions, Early justified the first on the grounds that Federals "invariably burned such works in the South, wherever they had penetrated"—notably those of John Bell of Tennessee, an old Whig who had run as the Constitutional Union candidate for the presidency in 1860. As for Chambersburg, by that point in the war Early had decided Federal outrages against Confederate civilians and their property had gone unanswered long enough. "[I]t was time to open the eyes of the people of the North," he wrote in his memoirs, "by an example in the way of retaliation."[26]

Emancipation visited the single greatest loss of property on the white South and seemingly placed in jeopardy a social structure built on white supremacy. Although scarcely repenting their slaveholding past and determined to reassert white control as soon as possible, most former Confederates nonetheless realized that Union victory circumscribed their options. The current of Western civilization ran strongly against them concerning slavery, and they knew an outspoken defense of the institution would discredit their Confederate experiment. Men such as Jefferson Davis and Alexander H. Stephens, who in 1860–61 had bluntly stated that slavery stood at the center of the sectional crisis, played down its importance and insisted that they had sought to protect their constitutional rights. Most white leaders also recognized that once the Radical Republicans had taken control of Reconstruction it made sense to give at least the appearance of treating black people fairly lest Congress pass more restrictive legislation.[27]

Early departed from former comrades who sought to accommodate themselves to changed circumstances regarding slavery and race. Unlike Davis and Stephens, he placed slavery at the center of the secession crisis: "The struggle for independence made by the Southern States," read the first sentence of *The Heritage of the South*, "grew out of questions of self government arising mainly in regard to the institution of African slavery." Early's private letters and public statements did not concede any positive effect of emancipation. In the spring of 1867, he manifested great unhappiness at the passing of the South's slave-based society: "A very small portion of the civilized world is guiltless in regard to the wrongs done our people, and I want to see all the nations punished for their folly & wicked intermeddling in regard to the institution of slavery, about the propriety, advantages and justice of which my opinion grows daily stronger." Foreigners who thought the Confederate government should have freed the slaves if it wanted help from abroad might note the experience of Don Quixote, who freed the galley slaves then had to defend himself against them. "What could the people of the South have done in the prosecution of the war," asked Early, "if 3,000,000 slaves had been turned loose among them and the whole labor system of the country deranged?"[28]

In 1875, he reaffirmed his support of slavery in a published letter declining an invitation to appear at a meeting of the Massachusetts Central Committee of the National Union Party: "However wrongful and unconstitutional we may regard the manner by which slavery was abolished, we all recognize the fact that it is abolished, and that its restoration, even if desirable, is a physical impossibility." Ten years later, Early learned that Thomas L. Rosser, a cavalry general who fought under him in the Shenandoah Valley, had called slavery a stain on the South. "I am only surprised," sputtered Early, "that I ever entertained the idea that he had any of the attributes of manhood."[29]

During a postwar era when white southerners usually muted their opinions about the "positive good" of slavery, Early drafted a remarkable analysis that rooted the institution in the ancient world and argued that charges of its sinfulness were a relatively recent phenomenon. Meticulously tracing the derivation of the word *slave* to prove that it should be equated with *servant* in the Bible, he quoted numerous Old and New Testament passages to bolster his conclusion that slavery and Christianity were entirely compatible. When Moses received the law of God through the Commandments, stated Early, the Lord protected property in menservants and maidservants through the tenth commandment: "Thus did that same God who had shown favor to Abraham, and Lot, and Isaac, and Jacob, and Job, all slave-holders, without once rebuking them because they held their fellow man in bondage, give his express sanction to the institution of domestic slavery, by positive law." He did note that Christianity brought one significant change: in the pre-Christian era masters had power over the slave's person as well as his life; Christianity revoked the latter and thus ameliorated the institution in settings such as the antebellum South.[30]

The specter of any challenge to absolute white supremacy elicited vigorous reactions from Early. He opposed the Fourteenth and Fifteenth Amendments; ridiculed southern Democrats who proposed alliances with black voters to defeat Republicans; and vehemently opposed the Readjuster movement in Virginia, which for a time in the late 1870s and early 1880s promised to unite segments of the state's white and black electorates behind a program that challenged the elitist, conservative, and white supremacist tenets of Early's thought. William H. Payne, a conservative Democrat who claimed Early as his mentor, habitually took pains to offer opinions he believed would please the older man. In late November 1879, Payne nicely captured why conservatives such as Early feared the Readjusters. "A permanent alliance between the negroes & mean white people is threatened," noted Payne in reference to the period of so-called black rule in South Carolina, "& there is every appearance of our returning to the hell from which Carolina has escaped." A prior attempt in Louisiana to fuse white and black voters had caused Early to send a sharp rebuke to P. G. T. Beauregard, who supported the idea as a way to drive out the Republicans. "[W]e only propose to accord to the colored people the political and civil rights guaranteed to them by our radical constitution," explained Beauregard in a fruitless effort to win Early over, "on condition that they will aid us in getting rid of these vagabonds who have been plundering us so unmercifully for the last five years."[31]

Early's 1875 letter to the Massachusetts Central Committee summed up his own unwavering position on white rule: "We . . . maintain that no good government can exist in the States of the South unless under the control of the white race, and we are resolutely opposed to all attempts to establish social equality between the whites and blacks." Professing a willingness to deal "kindly and justly" with black people, Early stressed that he never would accept any civil rights bill or the "Africanization" of any southern state.[32]

The depth of Early's aversion to black participation in Virginia's public affairs stood out in a controversy that erupted in October 1875. The debate centered on whether black militia units should be allowed to participate in ceremonies dedicating a statue to Stonewall Jackson in Richmond. Democratic Governor James L. Kemper, whose Confederate credentials included a wound received in Pickett's Charge at Gettysburg, arranged for the black men to march in the rear of the procession. Early strongly criticized the governor's decision, predicted that pictures of Lincoln and Fifteenth Amendment banners would be flaunted, and said anyone who marched with the black militia would be disgraced. Kemper responded that Jackson's widow and every other former Confederate soldier whom he had consulted gave their blessing. Moreover, the African Americans assured him they wished to honor Jackson because he had taught black children in a Sunday school in Lexington, Virginia, before the war. Any open controversy during the ceremonies would provide ammunition to the Republicans, stated Kemper, whereas a peaceful procession with the black units at the rear would be "best calculated to vindicate our White people against Radical lies." If Early planned to attend the ceremonies with the intention of talking to others "as you talk to me in your dispatch," concluded Kemper, "then for God's sake don't come at all." Unconcerned that he was out of step with most former Confederates, Early refused to endorse African-American participation and stayed away from the ceremonies.[33]

As one who venerated the Constitution for its protection of property and social stability, Early saw the entire period between April 1861 and the early months of 1877 as a time of outrages against the intent of the Founders. He often reiterated, as he did in a letter to former Confederate General Alexander R. Lawton in May 1885, that his conversion from unionism to secession had resulted from the "unconstitutional measures of Lincoln and his adherents." In January 1869, the *New York Times* quoted Early's reaction to Andrew Johnson's recent proclamation of amnesty to former Confederates. That proclamation, said Early, demonstrated the federal government's "*inability to hold any of us responsible,* under the Constitution and laws as they were, for our resistance to its usurpation." What of the Radical Republican claim that the South resorted to arbitration by arms and thus emerged from the war a conquered people subject to any federal legislation deemed necessary for reentry into the Union? "The Constitution created by sovereign states," argued Early, "whatever the powers delegated, could never have contemplated the possibility of one of those states being reduced to the condition of a conquered province." Federal intervention in domestic matters in the former Confederate states, including the deployment of soldiers in the South during peacetime, underscored the contempt with which Republican leaders viewed the Constitution.[34]

Yet Early continued to hope that the Constitution might serve, as before the war, to shield the white South from federal intrusions. He opposed the compromise of 1877—a bargain that impressed many white southerners as a sensible way to rid their section of federal troops—on the grounds that it weakened the Constitution. Early questioned whether Republican presidential candidate Rutherford B. Hayes, who received fewer popular and electoral votes than his Democratic opponent, should be inaugurated if it meant the Constitution had been violated. "What value will a constitution be to us, that is disregarded in the very organization of the government?" he asked Bradley T. Johnson. "If it is our sole reliance, then, we should fight to maintain its integrity, when its provisions are palpably violated in the inauguration of a man as President who has never been elected."[35]

Political views and activities provided other threads of continuity between Early's prewar and postwar careers. He explained in 1875 that although he had been a prewar Whig, he was "firmly convinced that the Democratic party, as at present organized, is the only one whose principles and policy can give any hope of a restoration of the rights of the States and a return of the Federal government to its ancient integrity." Standing with the white people of the state, as he put it, Early allied with Virginia's conservative Democrats and for more than a decade after his return from exile in Canada corresponded widely with various politicians. John Warwick Daniel, Fitzhugh Lee, and other younger ex-Confederates who would hold major state and national offices, as well as political leaders of an earlier generation, turned to Early for advice, took care to explain positions they knew would be at odds with his, and otherwise indicated that he was a man to be reckoned with in the state. He played an active role in opposing Readjuster efforts to reform the state debt in the 1870s, chastized Democrats who seemed to him overenthusiastic about placating the northern wing of the party, and always backed candidates most likely to protect the propertied classes.[36]

Associated with the Democratic conservative elite that held power in Virginia through much of the period between redemption and the early 1880s, he later reverted to his antebellum role as a conservative old Whig out of step with the majority of the electorate. A letter to William H. Payne in late 1885 indicated that he retained his antebellum idea of "patriotic submission." Fitzhugh Lee's dominant wing of the Democratic Party did not entirely suit Early, but he supported it because it represented the supremacy of white Virginians and thus was "absolutely necessary for the preservation of the interests and rights of the people, and all personal considerations should sink into insignificance in comparison with that."[37] In August 1884, Early underscored that he had not abandoned principles during his journey from conservative Whig and unionist to Confederate general and finally to postwar critic of the North and defender of the Lost Cause. "There is one thing I want you to learn and that is, that an old line Clay Whig makes the truest Democrat to be found in these times," he stated somewhat wistfully to a friend, "just as a sincere Union man in the days when men were wild about secession, made the truest and most persistent adherents of the cause of the South when the real contest came."[38]

Jubal Early offers a perfect example of someone whose opinions about political and social questions remained largely static through the tumultuous years of the mid–nineteenth century. Others adjusted their positions to meet new circumstances, but Early clung doggedly to his beliefs in the Constitution as it had been, the correctness of slavery, rule by a propertied elite, and the need for white supremacy in a biracial society. In its obituary for Early, the *Lynchburg News* compared him to an unlikely yet aptly chosen trio: "He was as eccentric as Randolph of Roanoke; as resolute and self-willed as Old Hickory himself; as relentless as Cromwell in the prompt dispatch of cruel duty."[39] The *News* also could have compared Early to someone who represented unchanging belief in a set of principles, for there lay the real secret to Jubal Early's life.

Notes

1. George H. Reese, ed., *Proceedings of the Virginia Secession Convention of 1861*, 4 vols. (Richmond, Va.: Virginia State Library, 1965), 4:58–59; Early to John

C. Breckinridge, March 27, 1867, original in the possession of William C. Davis. Mr. Davis kindly granted permission to quote from this document.

2. Early defined "patriotic submission" in remarks delivered at the Virginia secession convention on April 8, 1861. See Reese, ed., *Proceedings*, 3:357–58. Early's departures from the social conventions of his time—which included fathering several children by a white mistress in his hometown of Rocky Mount, Virginia— are beyond the scope of this paper; they are worth mentioning, however, as evidence of a pattern of acting in both public and private matters as he saw fit rather than as the majority dictated.

3. Thomas L. Connelly, *The Marble Man: Robert E. Lee and His Image in American Society* (New York: Alfred A. Knopf, 1977), 52–53; Thomas L. Connelly and Barbara L. Bellows, *God and General Longstreet: The Lost Cause and the Southern Mind* (Baton Rouge: Louisiana State University Press, 1982), 10.

4. Connelly, *Marble Man*, 54; Connelly and Bellows, *God and General Longstreet*, 10.

5. Charles C. Osborne, *Jubal: The Life and Times of General Jubal A. Early, CSA, Defender of the Lost Cause* (Chapel Hill, N.C.: Algonquin Books of Chapel Hill, 1992), 431; Gaines M. Foster, *Ghosts of the Confederacy: Defeat, the Lost Cause, and the Emergence of the New South* (New York: Oxford University Press, 1987), 5– 6, 60.

6. "1830 Personal Property Tax List, Franklin County, Virginia," *Virginia Appalachian Notes* 8 (February 1984): 4; extracts from Franklin County tax lists supplied by H. L. Hopkins of Rocky Mount, Virginia; R. H. Early, *The Family of Early, Which Settled upon the Eastern Shore of Virginia, and Its Connections with Other Families* (Lynchburg, Va.: Press of Brown-Morrison Co., 1920), 107–8; Elizabeth Seawell Hairston, *The Hairstons and Penns and Their Relatives* (Roanoke, Va.: Walters Printing and Manufacturing Co., 1940), 29; *De Bow's Review*, n.s. 1 (January 1855): 53.

7. Early to Joab Early, November 8, 1835, Scrapbook, Jubal A. Early Papers, Library of Congress, Washington, D.C. (hereafter cited as LC); Jubal A. Early, *Lieutenant General Jubal Anderson Early, C.S.A.: Autobiographical Sketch and Narrative of the War between the States* (1912; reprint, Wilmington, N.C.: Broadfoot Publishing Company, 1989), xliii. On Early and his regiment during the war with Mexico, see Lee A. Wallace, Jr., "The First Regiment of Virginia Volunteers 1846– 1848," *Virginia Magazine of History and Biography* 77 (January 1969): 46–77.

8. Early, *Lieutenant General Jubal Anderson Early*, xlii, xlvi; *Lynchburg Daily Virginian*, July 11, 1856, February 10, 1860; Reese, ed., *Proceedings*, 3:358; *Lynchburg News*, March 3, 1894.

9. Early, "To the Voters of Franklin, Henry & Patrick Counties," July 20, 1850, Scrapbook, Early Papers, LC.

10. *Lynchburg Daily Virginian*, September 9, 1850; Early, *Lieutenant General Jubal Anderson Early*, xlvi. For an excellent discussion of white southerners who shared Early's views about progress, see Eugene D. Genovese, *The Slaveholders' Dilemma: Freedom and Progress in Southern Conservative Thought, 1820–1860* (Columbia: University of South Carolina Press, 1992).

11. Early to William Ballard Preston, January 11, 1850, Mss1/P9267/d/422, Preston Family Papers, Virginia Historical Society, Richmond (hereafter cited as VHS); Reese, ed., *Proceedings*, 3:358; Jubal A. Early, *The Heritage of the South: A History of the Introduction of Slavery, Its Establishment from Colonial Times and Final Effect upon the Politics of the United States*, ed. R. H. Early (Lynchburg, Va.: Press of Brown-Morrison Co., 1915), 78. Published by his niece twenty-one years after Early's death, *The Heritage of the South* probably was written during the period 1865–70. R. H. Early stated in an editor's note that the manuscript had "lain unpublished during the passing of half a century, till passion having cooled and prejudice abated, there is no longer reason for clash from difference of feeling upon the subject."

12. Early, *Heritage*, 48, 61; *Lynchburg Daily Virginian*, July 11, 1856.

13. *Lynchburg Daily Virginian*, December 13, 1859.

14. The federal manuscript census returns for 1840, 1850, and 1860 show no slave property for Early; the 1846 personal property tax list for Franklin County includes among his holdings one slave over twelve years old. In her editor's note for *The Heritage of the South*, R. H. Early remarked that "The author was never an investor in slaves, although he always possessed a negro servant."

15. Early, *Heritage*, 51–52.

16. Jubal A. Early, *A Memoir of the Last Year of the War for Independence, in the Confederate States of America, Containing an Account of the Operation of His Commands in the Years 1864 and 1865* (Toronto: Lovell and Bibson, 1866), viii–ix.

17. *Lynchburg Virginian*, February 7, 8, 12, 1861; Washington Dickinson to Early, January 17, 1861, Early Papers, LC.

18. Reese, ed., *Proceedings*, 1:428.

19. Ibid., 3:723, 4:167, 3:287.

20. Ibid., 4:167, 540.

21. Ibid., 4:168, 329; T. B. Greer to Jubal A. Early, April 25, 1861, Early Papers, LC; Early to John Letcher, May 2, 1861, File Mar–25–1, folder E-F, VHS.

22. "Virginia's Ordinance of Secession," *Confederate Veteran* 40 (April 1932): 128 (reproducing Early's commentary about why he signed the ordinance); Early, *Memoir*, iii–iv.

23. Sarah Strickler Fife diary, March 7, 1865, Alderman Library, University of Virginia, Charlottesville; John Cheves Haskell to "Dear Ma," March 5, 1865, Rachel Susan Cheves Papers, Perkins Library, Duke University, Durham, North Carolina (hereafter cited as DU).

24. Martin F. Schmitt, ed., "An Interview with General Jubal A. Early in 1889," *Journal of Southern History* 11 (November 1945): 562; Early, *Lieutenant General Jubal Anderson Early,* xliv.

25. Early, *Memoir,* 51, 53; Early to "the Editor of the State," [June 1882], Early to J. Randolph Tucker, February 22, 1886, Early Papers, LC.

26. Early to [J?] Fraise Richard, May 7, 1886, Jubal A. Early Papers, New-York Historical Society, New York; Early, *Memoir,* 71.

27. For useful discussions of how former Confederates handled the issue of slavery, see Foster, *Ghosts,* and Connelly, *Marble Man.*

28. Early, *Heritage,* 11, 116; Early to John C. Breckinridge, March 27, 1867, original in the possession of William C. Davis.

29. Early to Russell H. Conwell, August 30, 1875, clipping from unidentified newspaper; Early to William H. Payne, August 22, 1885, Early Papers, LC.

30. Jubal A. Early, "Slavery," 1–5, 9, 13–15, undated manuscript in Scrapbook, Early Papers, LC.

31. William H. Payne to Early, November 14, 1879, P. G. T. Beauregard to Early, July 17, 1873, Early Papers, LC. For analyses of conservative Democrats and the Readjuster movement, see Jack P. Maddex, Jr., *The Virginia Conservatives, 1867–1879: A Study in Reconstruction Politics* (Chapel Hill: University of North Carolina Press, 1970), and James Tice Moore, *Two Paths to the New South: The Virginia Debt Controversy, 1870–1883* (Lexington: University Press of Kentucky, 1974).

32. Early to Russell H. Conwell, August 30, 1875, clipping from unidentified newspaper, Early Papers, LC.

33. James L. Kemper to Early, October 23, 26, 1875, Early Papers, LC.

34. Early to A. R. Lawton, May 27, 1885, Early Papers, LC; *New York Times,* January 17, 1869; Early, *Heritage,* 117.

35. Early to Bradley T. Johnson, January 5, 1877, Bradley T. Johnson Papers, DU.

36. Early to Russell H. Conwell, August 30, 1875, clipping from unidentified newspaper, Early Papers, LC. For representative examples of Early's political correspondence, see John Warwick Daniel to Early, August 21, 1874, Fitzhugh Lee to Early, May 9, 1875, and R. E. Wither to Early, May 15, 1876, Early Papers, LC.

37. Early to William H. Payne, December 4, 1885, Mss1/H9267/a/9, Hunton Family Papers, VHS.

38. Early to J. Randolph Tucker, August 8, 1884, Tucker Family Papers, Southern Historical Collection, University of North Carolina, Chapel Hill.

39. *Lynchburg News,* March 6, 1894.

Army Post Office of the Chief Ambulance Officer, 9th Army, Petersburg, Virginia, August, 1864. Courtesy State Historical Society
of Wisconsin Whi (x3)14442.

The Common Soldier
of the Civil War

Joseph T. Glatthaar

"THERE IS NOT MUCH glory in soldiering to one who has his mind set
on a life of higher usefulness," sighed one frustrated Yankee veteran. "For a man to enjoy the service, he must not be averse to much
strong drink, must not be encumbered with morals & must possess
an insatiable appetite for confusion," quipped a Union soldier. "My
dear cousin, are you not tired of war?" wondered a Confederate soldier of three years. "The life I lead is so very different to that in
which I was reared, it is so antagonistic to my nature, that sometimes
when I think of its probable duration for four or five years to come,
I am nearly overcome by its depressing weight." Sometimes, he elaborated, he "would almost welcome the bullet which would terminate
so much trouble," but such would be an "unmanly" act. He still retained a powerful commitment to Southern independence, "Yet there
are times when the heart is sick, sick, sick of this life in the wilderness, this absence of pleasures, comforts, friends, of the beauties of
social and family circles, this weary pilgrimage of freedom!" In con-
currence, a Federal infantryman announced, "I don't like the Service & the war & shall be glad enough when peace shall be proclaimed
& I can return again to my books & peaceful pursuits, for all that I
am in it to the end."[1]

They were but four of the millions of young men who responded to the call of their governments, 2.25 million on behalf of the Union and nearly one million defending the Confederacy. Conscripts and substitutes for drafted men comprised a fraction of those who rallied around the flag. Almost all soldiers were volunteers. They entered military service wide eyed, anticipating glory and rapid success, and instead experienced hardship and heartache.

Like the America from which they came, most soldiers were from farming or rural backgrounds. Generally, they were young, unmarried males, although perhaps one hundred women served without anyone knowing—or at least publicizing—it. The Federal army had more skilled workers, clerks, professional men, and factory workers than did the Confederates because northern society had more skilled laborers. Approximately 400,000 men in the Union army (about 20 percent of the total) were foreign born. But that figure represented society as a whole: 20 percent of all northerners were foreign born. Literacy, too, reflected the general population: northerners tended to be better educated, but well-educated southerners served as privates, as did well-schooled Yankees. And both sides had their share of marginally literate or wholly illiterate soldiers.

Few recruits were worldly. A twenty-mile circle radiating from home would frequently circumscribe their world. The pace of life, too, was slower, the product of a less-complex existence. Yet these men were a more directed, industrious, self-reliant lot. They lived in an age when no safety net existed, when people worked until they died unless family members had the financial ability to support them in old age. Men and women of the mid–nineteenth century possessed a peculiar blend of idealism, individualism, and practicality. They depended on their own labor and judgment for survival, fostering confidence in their own decision-making abilities. Accustomed to forming their own opinions about matters, and unaccustomed to regimentation or significant intrusions by government, their sense of independence proved both the boon and the bane of their military existence.

Because almost all soldiers were volunteers, and because they decided for themselves on important issues, their commitment to their cause was unusually strong. Some certainly deserted ranks and others shirked duties, and Southerners ultimately capitulated to the Union, but the overwhelming majority endured frightful hardships for years while at their posts, and the Confederacy yielded with great reluctance in the face of overwhelming Federal strength. Even amid the squalor of the Reconstruction years, ex-Rebels continued to resist Federal directives for change, and they were eventually able to shape and mold a postwar world much to their liking.

At the root of secession and the war was slavery. Confederate President Jefferson Davis asked fellow Southerners, "Will you be slaves or will [you] be independent? ... Will you consent to be robbed of your property" or "strike back bravely for liberty, property, honor and life?" Secession, Davis believed, was necessary to protect against a movement to make "property in slaves so insecure as to be comparatively worthless." Vice President Alexander Stephens insisted that the Northern threat to slavery was the "immediate cause of the late rupture and present revolution." The Southern Confederacy, Stephens argued, rejected the notion that all men are created equal: "Its foundations are laid, its cornerstone rests, upon the great truth that the negro is not equal to the white man; that slavery, subordination to the superior race, is his natural and normal condition."[2]

When southerners claimed that they were seceding and going to war in defense of their "rights," they were defending their right to own property, their right to control and employ that property without harassment and endangerment from fellow citizens, and their right to take that property safely with them anywhere they saw fit. One Alabamian, promising to "fight forever, rather than submit to freeing negroes among us," insisted that the South went to war for "rights and property bequeathed to us by our ancestors." The aim of the Founding Fathers had been the protection of civil liberties, including ownership of private property. Confederates were merely defending those rights.[3]

After the war, southerners adopted a different tune. Few of them would have endorsed the blunt assertion of W. P. Heflin, an unreconstructed Rebel: "The negro was the main object and only cause of the greatest calamity that ever befell the American independence." Most had come to contend that secession and the war revolved around states' rights. But even then, this argument was a blanket for protection of the right to own and utilize slaves freely.[4]

Attuned as they were to distinctions between slavery and freedom, secessionists believed they could not submit to Union interference with their rights over that property. Otherwise, they themselves would become enslaved. "It is the *duty* of every man woman & child who can understand the difference between Liberty and Vassalism, to do all in their power no matter what that may be," explained a soldier. Union troops became tyrants, hirelings, Hessians, mercenaries who sought to suppress the rights of southerners. Slaveholders and nonslaveholders alike could unite under this banner—in either case, without civil liberties, people were nothing more than slaves to others.[5]

The Confederate States of America became the final preserve for civil rights. It was the "New Jerusalem," explained a soldier, "the last hope of free Government." Surely a just God and the inevitable progress of mankind would sustain an attempt to preserve freedom. *"We are right!"* proclaimed a Mississippian, "and sooner or later *right* must triumph!"[6]

Once the Union declared the Southern states in rebellion, the dispute escalated into an armed conflict. In defense of the Confederacy, vowed one volunteer, "I shall fight like I was standing at the threshold of my door fighting against robbers and savages for the defense of my wife & family." Northern violations of Southern rights, the refusal to let Southerners leave the Union peaceably, and the threat against them and their families melded to enflame passions against what had been countrymen. "The acme of a Southern soldier's ambition consists in the fervent hope, that he may be afforded the earliest practicable chance of crossing bayonets, with the mercenaries of a Despotic tyrant, who has without a cause forced upon him the alternative of resistance or servilism, & drive him in confusion and dismay from the sacred soil of his sunny South," explained a wordy Rebel.[7]

Northerners took up arms to preserve the Union. Generations later, that cause seemed ambiguous, but to the men and women of the Northern states, the concept was clear. The Union was eighty years old, the world's great experiment in democratic republicanism. A model for other nations, the United States served as a haven for the oppressed. Northerners believed that by preserving the Union they were merely carrying the torch for the Founding Fathers, with a sacred obligation to pass it on to the next generation. It was "the beacon of light of liberty & freedom to the human race," insisted an Indiana sergeant.[8]

Although the Constitution stated nothing about secession, the practice trampled an inherent principle of the government—all would abide by the results of a legal election. Secession as a precedent could unravel any union and undercut the democratic elements of any government, a lesson not lost on Confederates, who created their union inviolate. As one Federal noted, "constitutional liberty cannot survive the loss of unity in the government."[9]

The government, moreover, played a more essential role in the eyes of northerners. It represented a system, a blend of civil liberties and economic possibilities. The United States was a nation of genuine opportunity, without formal social levels—a land of the middle class, with a sort of universal value system. Only in the United States could a laborer elevate himself peacefully to the presidency, as Abraham Lincoln did. The government's mission was to protect and preserve rights and to ensure a fair, competitive environment with real opportunity. Qualities and values such as intelligence, honesty, and hard work would ensure success. In that context, many northerners found slavery extremely offensive. Slavery gave the slaveholder an unfair advantage and impeded opportunity. To northerners, slavery was a threat to free labor.

No doubt, few northerners went to war over slavery. Unusual was the Yankee who wrote home, "I tell the boys right to their face I am in the war for the freedom of the slave. When they talk about the saving of the Union I tell them that is Dutch to me." While many northerners did not like the peculiar institution, they also did not like blacks. And they certainly were not willing to go to war to free the slaves. "The Constitution & the Union are enough for me to fight for," explained a Massachusetts captain.[10]

Yet many northerners believed that the slave states had dominated the government and that there was a giant "slave conspiracy" to retain power. In a prewar commencement address entitled "Will the American Experiment Fail?" a future soldier described the Fugitive Slave Law as "repugnant to the cherished principles of Northern Freedom, & is calculated to awaken the most determined hostility & resentment." Another viewed secession as an act in response to "their lossing control of the government, and with it, executive patronage, and the emoluments of office, the humiliation, proud aristocrats that they are, to be governed by a 'Mudsill.'"[11]

The North was free, progressive, educated, economically vibrant, a region bursting with opportunity. Northerners perceived the South as closed, backward, uneducated, economically retarded, a region with opportunities solely for the wealthy. For other southerners, it was hopeless. Northerners believed that they were fighting the good fight, protecting the Union, civil liberties, and possibilities. "Sure as right will in the end triumph over wrong," elaborated a Yankee soldier, "so sure will the principles of Freedom, free thought, free speech, free press, free schools, and free *government* for which we fight, & ask *God's* help, tryumph in the end over Slavery, ignorance, and tyranny and *brutishness.*"[12]

People on both sides rallied around their governments. Husbands begged wives for permission to enlist; sons pleaded with parents to let them join; women shamed loved ones into going. Some young men ran off to the army without parental consent. All were caught in the furor of the moment. "If a fellow wants to go with a girl now he had better enlist," commented an Indiana boy. "The girls sing 'I am Bound to be a Soldier's Wife or Die an Old Maid.'" Fresh enlistees reminded sisters to accept only soldiers as spouses. "My dear sisters, i as an elder brother want you not to name no young man [as your husband] whoo will not volunteer any fight for the [rights] of his country," commanded a Virginian, "but wait and take one whoo has faught for liberties and freddom of thier country."[13]

Since both sides recruited units on a local level, the enlistment process often whipped a community into a frenzy. They took on peculiar names—the "Invincibles," the "Thrashers," the "Yankee-Killers," and the "Southern Rejectors of Old Abe." Many a heart was broken and a curse was uttered early in the war when locals learned that the government had no room for their volunteers. As the war dragged on, both the Union and the Confederacy struggled to increase troop strength. At the beginning, however, more volunteers turned out than either government could accept. For the "lucky" ones, there was a community picnic or dinner, with presentation of a flag and a raucous send-off.[14]

The initial parting was difficult for most families. Many men had never before separated from their wives, and seldom did unattached sons move out of their parents' households. But patriotism overruled personal considerations, and few anticipated the conflict would last long. "Be of good cheer & keep a stout heart—My dearest best wife," a Georgian wrote. "If I fall or die don't grieve over me as one entirely lost—You will know that you interposed no selfish objections to your husband doing his duty & I would were I a woman vastly prefer to be a true man's widow than some men's wives."[15]

Screening of prospective recruits was perfunctory at best. In many cases, a few thumps on the chest by a physician comprised a physical. Later in the war, when some people preferred to avoid military service, individuals demanded more rigorous examinations. But early in the war, few doctors were willing to disappoint an enthusiastic volunteer by turning him away. Even minors swore the oath without objections. A convenient practice was for an underage candidate to slip into his shoe a piece of paper with the number eighteen written on it. That way, when asked whether he met the minimum age qualification, the lad could honestly say he was "over" eighteen. Locals knew better but looked the other way.

Since few volunteers had previous military experience, soldiers selected officers from their own ranks. Individuals fighting for civil liberties were not likely to waive their rights in choosing superiors in rank. As one Confederate explained, "Men are as intelligent in camp as at home, and can vote as intelligently for their officers as they can for members of Congress." Election day was usually quite an event. Candidates frequently curried favor by plying the men with whiskey, which made for a raucous affair, regardless of the outcome.[16]

Despite the differences in motivation of Northern and Southern boys, the common organization, tactics, weapons, and problems tended to create a commonality to their experiences in military service. Both sides utilized essentially the same unit sizes and tactics manuals. A full-strength infantry regiment consisted of approximately 1,000 men, a couple of hundred more for a cavalry regiment. Slightly more than one hundred soldiers composed an artillery battery. Such units often functioned at less than 50 percent strength. Early in the war, troops employed a wide range of firearms, but after a year or two armies became more uniform. A .58-caliber Springfield or a .577-caliber Enfield became weapons of choice for infantrymen. These guns were extremely accurate at several hundred yards, firing huge rounds of soft lead that traveled at a low muzzle velocity and inflicted gaping wounds. Cavalrymen found carbines more useful than sabers, and by the later stages of the war many Union horsemen packed seven-shot repeating carbines. Although they lacked the effective range of a rifled musket, carbines were smaller and easier to handle on horseback. Artillery employed both smoothbore and rifled guns, with the smoothbore Napoleon the most common. Standard artillery ammunition included canister for just a few hundred yards and solid shots and shells for up to a mile and more.

Men entered military service eager to meet the enemy in battle. Yet the reality of Civil War soldiering was lengthy stays in camp, with periodic and demanding campaigns. In time, soldiers on both sides equated their positions to slaves—deprived of freedom, incapable of controlling their own time, and unable to make decisions for themselves.

Drill and discipline consumed part of the day, as officers, many of them learning alongside their troops, attempted to impose rigor and structure on resistant soldiers. In the Civil War, units practiced tactical maneuvers that their officers would order them to execute in battle. It was vital, therefore, that the men mastered each drill. At first, army ways excited volunteers, but repetition bred boredom and contempt. Rain or shine except in the height of winter, men drilled anywhere from two to five hours per day. Additional chores included picket and guard duty, collecting firewood, and cooking.

The rest of the day was for the soldiers as long as they remained in camp. With substantial free time available, the irrepressible nature of young males appeared. As one Confederate shrewdly noticed, "Common soldiers by name, however, are often times very uncommon—like common sense." Game, mischievous, creative, unconcerned about consequences, dominated by a sense of indestructibility, and beyond the restrictions of normal civilization, soldiers embarked on a host of activities to entertain themselves that would have been inconceivable in peacetime.[17]

"Our life now is very monotonous," explained one soldier. "The boys resort to various expedients to wear away time, the chief one of which is teasing each other." Only their imaginations limited the range and depth of pranks, jokes, and taunts. One Yankee thought it would be comical to start a brushfire and rush to a commanding position so that he could view his friends battle the rattlesnakes that were driven into camp. Another fellow fired a few rounds into the adjacent camp just to watch everyone scurry for cover in fright. His company commander did not find it as amusing, though, when authorities placed him under arrest for failing to control his men. In Sherman's army, a favorite trick was to ignite sap from a pine tree under which a soldier napped. Sap would then ooze out of the tree, gluing the man to it. A crowd of onlookers would then awaken the man and observe the panic on his face when he tried to break free.[18] One Confederate battery pulled a prank on a comrade by staging a phony election for a vacant lieutenancy. The winner had no clue about the scam, which the troops maintained for three days. "He even went so far as to have bars put on his collar and put on airs generally," a soldier gleefully recorded. "He was the greatest fool I ever saw."[19]

State rivalries and sectionalism prompted considerable taunting and jokes. In Southern armies, the competitiveness was mostly among states; among Union troops, it was more east versus west. North Carolinians liked to boast that they lived in a "valley of humility between two mountains of conceit [Virginia and South Carolina]." Virginians called their southern neighbors Tarheels. As some North Carolinians passed by, a Virginian called out, "Any more tar down in the Old North State, boys?"

"No, not a bit. Old Jeff's bought it all up."

"Is that so? What is he going to do with it?"

"He's going to put it in you'ns heels to make you stick better in the next fight."[20]

Eastern men in the Union army referred to Sherman's army as "Sherman's Greasers," "Slouch Hats," "Swamp Angels," and "Thieves." Troops in the western army responded by accusing others of being "paper collars," "featherbeds," and "white gloves," suggesting that Sherman's men did all the work and the Army of the Potomac simply paraded.[21]

Officers were especially appealing targets for harassment and pranks. Reared in a democratic society, undisciplined citizen-soldiers were extremely sensitive to rank and behavior. Officers who took themselves too seriously or lorded it over their prewar friends and neighbors paid a high price for their conduct. Standard treatment included troops discrediting the offender by misbehaving before superior officers. Other times men perpetrated acts like shaving the tail of an officer's horse, an embarrassing penalty to an individual who loved to look the part of an officer. Soldiers frequently subjected unpopular officers to catcalls. "Take them mice out of your mouth—take 'em out," soldiers jeered at an officer with a mustache. "No use to say they aint thar—see their tails hanging out." Nicknames, too, were popular. One regiment called its major "A. No. 1." No doubt, the officer thought of it as a compliment, but troops had a different meaning: the *A* stood for *ass*.[22]

To annoy officers, amuse themselves, and remind their leaders who was really in charge, some Mississippians collected horns and blew them. When the colonel ordered them silent, the soldiers interpreted that as a challenge. One company began tooting its horns, and as soon as an officer quieted them down, another company picked up the task. The officer raced from company to company, trying to silence the trumpeting, but it was hopeless. The soldiers made their statement.[23]

Cavalrymen, too, were particularly popular targets for abuse. Compared to infantrymen or artillerists, their service was not as demanding physically, and the loss of life and limb was much less. Officers joked about offering rewards to see the body of a dead cavalryman because they were so rare. To a horseman with big, expensive boots, the regimental cry was, "Come out of them boots—Come out!—too soon to go into winter quarters I know you are thar see your arms sticking out." Such ridicule sometimes led to violence. When an Irish infantryman requested that a long-beaked cavalryman turn his head to the side so that the army could pass, he sparked a brawl.[24]

Music was a the chief form of organized entertainment. Regimental bands serenaded high-ranking officers, which benefited everyone within earshot. Around campfires, clusters of soldiers struck up tunes occasionally, lending their voices to such favorites as "John Brown's Body," "Dixie," and "Home, Sweet Home." While in winter quarters, men formed troupes and performed plays and concerts. One Confederate burlesque outfit included a striptease, with soldiers shedding women's garments in comical fashion.[25]

More solitary pursuits included reading and letter writing. Newspapers, Victor Hugo, Walter Scott, various military histories, and the Bible were army favorites. Family and friends yearned for reports from the front, and men in uniform felt an unusual burden. While campaigning, they had much to tell and no opportunity to write. When they hung around camp for weeks on end, they had plenty of time and little to tell. And sometimes they did things that they probably should not tell, as one confused Federal wrote: "you sed in one of your last letters to me that I could not write to menny letters but if you knew how I am cutting round a rebe girle I recon you would not want meney more of my letters but I shant say a worde a boute it so you will think I am all rite. Well never minde we are going to leave heare in a few days so I will forget my rebe girle and be as good as ever."[26]

Soldiers hundreds of miles from home longed to hear news from their loved ones. Nothing was more agonizing than the interminable wait between missives. "Tell me which or when all my correspondents died," wondered a lonesome Michigander. When mail finally did arrive, men were euphoric: "I can live a month without eating now," exclaimed a Minnesotan, "I have got five letters from my wife." As one corporal explained, "Nothing will make the heart of a soldier glader than to receive some token from home no difference how small."[27]

Correspondence, however, proved a temporary fix. It did not replace the longing to be with family and friends. "On my couch when deep sleep has fallen on others," confessed a Georgian to his wife, "I often shed tears at the cruel separation that divides me from my loved ones." Until military service intervened, many soldiers had never spent a night away from their wives or parents. The thrill of army life carried them through the first few weeks, but soon the realities of separation began to sink in. Wyman Folsom, a seventeen-year-old Minnesotan, extracted a promise from his mother that she would pray for him every night at nine o'clock. After more than a year in uniform, the pangs for reunion grew more and more potent. "You dont Know how much your young soldier thinks of you," Folsom confessed. "I am sick as thunder I shall bust if I have to stay in the Army two years longer." Leaves of absence offered soldiers a chance to return home, as long as enemy soldiers had not overrun the area. By 1864, however, neither government exhibited much willingness to grant furloughs liberally. "A man has to be $9/10$ dead himself and then certify all his friends, family & acquaintences are about to breathe their last, before a leave is granted him," explained a Federal soldier. Homesickness was one of the great contributors to the high absent-without-leave and desertion rates for both sides.[28]

For consolation during these trying times, many soldiers turned to religion. In both armies, religious revivals percolated up from the ranks periodically, during bad times and good. Religion provided men with the consolation that the loss of comrades and perhaps even their own lives would not be in vain. It convinced them that God would shield them in their hour of need. Religion served as a link to the world back home and memories of peace and happiness. While reinforcing their sense of the justice of their cause, revivals reminded soldiers that God would aid them in their hour of need. "Our cause is a just one," a Georgian explained to his sister. "God is a just God; therefore we must win."[29] Outpourings of fervor and violent quakes in the conversion process proved an excellent release for frustrations and tensions. Psychologically, revival participants felt an enormous burden removed from their shoulders.

As religion worked to rejuvenate morals and establish a nexus with peacetime life, other factors tempted troops to wander down the road to eternal damnation. Away from more traditional society and hidden from parental and spousal observation, soldiers' ethics began to decay. The government had removed young men from society, placed uniforms on their backs, paid them and given them three meals per day, and required them to endure seemingly limitless periods of boredom replaced briefly by a few hours of terror and bloodshed. War called upon these men to cast aside one of society's greatest taboos, the killing of fellow human beings, and witness the destruction of lives and property on an unprecedented scale. Such an environment inevitably led to a decline in moral conduct of many of the men. "Camp life is a miserable life if a person wishes to do what is right and tries to get his mind composed," grumbled a soldier to his parents. "There is so much noise and vain and vulgar talk it appears like he cant keep his mind on one thing long at a time." Profanity, gambling, drinking, and even excursions to bawdy houses were commonplace in military life. "Few there are who have escaped the contagious effects of being mixed up with the vile and low," complained a soldier to his mother and sisters. "All grades of society and character are here blended indiscriminately together. The bad are not reformed while the good are made bad."[30]

Amid such stagnation and misbehavior, hardships and frustration abounded in camp. Instead of whipping the enemy, Union soldiers were lying around throughout the North. One man wrote home of the heavy casualties the "Bloody 6th" Ohio Cavalry inflicted. "It was a very *hard fought-battle; of the Enemy. One-hundred were killed,* and several taken *prisoners of war.* . . . The boys killed 100 old and young *rats* 75 very large ones and run some more into holes in the ground." Losses were not from Confederate lead but accidental wounds and diseases that raced through camp and took fearful tolls. As one soldier concluded, "there is more reality than poetry in a life on the Tented field."[31]

Accustomed to wholesome meals of fresh meat and vegetables, farm boys now had to gag down worm-infested hardtack, green-tinged beef or slimy pork, coarse cornmeal, and dessicated or dehydrated vegetables. Fresh fruits and vegetables were luxuries. Illnesses due to an unbalanced diet were regular features in Civil War armies. Had soldiers not received occasional care packages from home, the problem would have reached epidemic proportions.

Despite the suspect quality, a full ration provided ample caloric intake. Unfortunately, shortages frequently forced officers to issue reduced rations. Late in the war, Confederates around Petersburg cut back to two meals per day, and rations occasionally lacked meat; most times, soldiers received only one-quarter pound of meat per day. The corn bread, complained a soldier in Lee's army, "looks like a pile of cow dung baked in the sun." It was so hard that "I could nock down a cow with a pone of it." Federals, too, went hungry. "To day they issued 3 ears of Corn a piece. I am getting to look quite mulish, my ears ar getting very long; packing us & feeding us on Mule rations fetches them out wonderfully. I think in a few days I can put to shame (in the way of ears) any thing of the mule kind," joked a Yankee. It was small wonder that soldiers on both sides plundered orchards and were such expert marksmen when livestock charged them.[32]

Clothing shortages plagued all soldiers during the Civil War. Early in the war, green troops regularly packed too much. Veterans joked that you could track a column of recruits by the discarded clothing that littered the roadsides. In time, they learned to carry only the necessities. Without previous experience, they could not conceive that campaigning would teach them to throw away all excess baggage, as one soldier wrote home: "I shall have to come down to nothing but a rubber blanket before a great while. I haven't thrown away that Bible yet but I'm afraid it will have to go, when you are on the march continually day & night every ounce tells like thunder." But with no room for spares, rich and poor alike suffered from want of adequate garments when items wore out. It was one of war's great levelers. "Thir is pleanty of lawyers and Doctors hear barefooted and nearly necked that used to ware broad cloth and wouldent hardly speek to a comon man," commented a Virginian. "My boots were utterly worn out," the son of a Confederate senator reported. "My pantaloons were all one big hole as the Irishman would say; my coat was like a beggar's and my hat was actually falling to pieces." At times, men attended inspections without pants, hats, and shirts because theirs had worn out and the government had failed to issue new ones. As one soldier explained, "Such constant marching on rough, rocky roads, and sleeping on the bare ground, will naturally wear out the best shoes and thickest of pants."[33]

Shoes were a particularly serious problem during the war. Marching was the primary mode of transportation, and macadamized thoroughfares, rocky dirt roads, snow and mud, and streams and rivers tore up shoes and boots. "We are war worn and foot sore," protested a Confederate in the middle of an extensive campaign. "My feet are blistered top & bottom & my boots nearly entirely gone. One more day's tramp & I shall be in the condition of hundreds in our army—barefoot." Men straggled because they lacked footwear, and on several occasions the outcome of campaigns might have changed if all troops had satisfactory shoes. "I am barefoot and my feet are extremely sore," complained a Yankee, "when I step on them the blood oozes from the bottoms in such profusion that if I was on the snow I could be easily tracked." At Fredericksburg in December 1862 many barefoot Confederates left such tracks.[34]

Armies attempted every conceivable method to obtain shoes for the men. They even assembled cobblers from within the ranks to stitch together cowhides for foot cover during the winter months.

When the army was unable to provide for him, one resourceful bare-footed soldier had a comrade sketch the outline of his foot and sent it home to his father to have "Cowan in the village" make him a new pair. "Tell him to make them a little loose as this paper is the exact measure," he explained.[35]

Living on meager diets and inadequately clad and shod, it was no surprise that soldiers succumbed in astounding numbers to illness and disease. Governments brought together hundreds of thousands of men, most of them from rural backgrounds, and exposed them to illnesses that most had never experienced before. Armies were massive cities—the Army of Northern Virginia had more people in it than any southern city in 1860 except New Orleans—and often lacked satisfactory water supplies and waste disposal practices. Diseases roared through camps, passed through water or food supplies to a population already weak from unbalanced diets and excessive exposure. Poor sanitation magnified the problem.

Early in the war, childhood diseases that farm boys had dodged at home roared through camps with a vengeance. Measles, mumps, chicken pox, and smallpox took a terrible toll on soldiers. It was not unusual for 50 percent of a regiment to fall ill with these maladies.

Inadequate sanitary practices only compounded the awful situation. Undisciplined troops responded anywhere to nature's call. "On rolling up my bed this morning," a soldier penned home, "I found I had been lying in—I wont say what—something that didn't smell like milk and peaches." All too often soldiers contaminated their water supply by urinating or defecating upstream or by grazing livestock there. Typhoid fever, dysentery (bloody flux), diarrhea (Virginia or Tennessee quickstep or the flux), cholera, and other ailments spread like wildfire through this medium.[36]

Civil War soldiers were not terribly tidy in camp. They used sinks improperly and failed to police living areas. Dead bodies or refuse baked or rotted in the hot sun, attracting lice, fleas, flies, gnats, and rats and spreading sickness everywhere. After the engagement at First Manassas, Confederate soldiers camped on the battlefield amid corpses and dead animals. Many Rebels drew water from Bull Run, despite bodies and carcasses cluttering the waterway. Sickness quickly reached epidemic proportions, and units had to relocate a mile or two to the rear for health reasons. In South Carolina, a captain filed a protest against the insects that overwhelmed him. "The nits gnats and sandflies together with mosquitoes and house flies are simply terrific especially when there is no breeze to blow them away," he moaned. "I tried to write up my company books and found it almost impossible even if I scratched and slapped until my fingers and skin were alike sore." As a last resort, he bought a box of cigars and had enlisted men come into his tent, smoke the cigars, and puff the smoke at him, which he found reasonably effective.[37]

Soldiers readily joked about omnipresent mosquitoes. At that time physicians did not know that mosquitoes carried malaria, believing instead that the cause was miasmas emanating from the ground. Although these pests were almost always bothersome to soldiers, they were more a source of sarcastic humor than a health worry. At Fort Jackson, Louisiana, a black sergeant wrote, "we are attacked on the right and left flank by millions upon millions of mosquitoes, which, by night, charge upon us, front and rear, and cause us to beat a hasty retreat to our nets for protection from their daggers, which they plunge with a will." To the north in Tennessee along the Mississippi River a surgeon good-naturedly complained, "the Misquitoes, failing to drag my hands from the paper, and now trying to cut my head off in the same way that a large tree might be cut down by boring auger holes.—I fear I shall have to flee for my life." Malaria killed tens of thousands, yet it was one of the few maladies that Civil War physicians could treat with some positive results.[38]

For the seriously ill or injured, authorities established hospitals, which usually were overcrowded. Nurses, who did more for healing than anyone else because they kept patients clean, were in short supply, and soldiers often served as inadequate substitutes. One Memphis hospital posted rules that included, "Nurses are authorized to require any patient *spitting* on the floor to clean it up and patients are also authorized to exact the same of nurses." The fact that hospitals had to establish such regulations did not bode well for the care they provided. Medicines were also in short supply, mercifully in most cases. Physicians tried their best but were powerless in the face of nature's strength. With few exceptions, they might just as well have been witch doctors. Joseph Lister did not make his discovery about germs until after the war. Either an individual had the constitutional strength to fight off the disease, or he perished. Perhaps 400,000 or more yielded to illness in the war.[39]

Campaigning also did not prove to be as enjoyable as many of the men had imagined. Most had envisioned themselves delivering a crushing blow to the enemy and ending the strife in short order. Few had considered sore, blistered feet, exposure to all the elements, and moldy or worm-infested rations. Water and mud saturated fabrics and made loads almost unbearable. "It rained steadily all night and as the water persisted in running under our beds all night we found ourselves this morning a trifle the worse for wear," noted one Yankee. "Our blankets, tents and overcoats were saturated with mud and water which made our loads exceedingly heavy. I estimated mine as follows, wool blanket twenty-five hundred pounds. Overcoat one ton, shelter tents fifteen hundred pounds. other traps a trifle."[40]

None of the soldiers had thought that they would do so much campaigning with no idea where they were going and what the plan was. "If you want to find a *'Know Nothingism'* in its purity," an enlisted man wrote home, "just come into the army and you can find it, Col. down to private." And as the weeks became months and even years, familiar sounds and experiences of military life replaced those of the civilian world. One New Yorker described it well when he wrote, "Our experience during the past year has dispelled all the novelty, mystery & glory of a soldier's life. The rattle of the drum is more familiar to our ears than ever was the school bell & the booming of cannon accompanied by the howling of the shell, as it approaches us commands rather less emotion than we were want to bestow to the firing of blanks at a fourth of July celebration in Chatauqua." The hardships were almost intolerable. As one Rebel soldier and parent confessed, "Did I think our precious boy would ever be required to undergo what my fortune has cast upon me I think I would greatly prefer to give him up as dearly as I love him and as completely as our hopes are centred upon him." Another notified his father, "I hope you will stay at home for you could not stand it it is too hard a life. . . . I would advise all friends unless they wish to live like negroes to stay at home I know if there is another war this chicken won be *thar* when they enlist."[41]

Early in the struggle, Union and Confederate soldiers pleaded for an opportunity to engage in battle. One Alabamian noticed that whenever men could hear distant guns or cannon fire, they cursed "loudly & deeply" over their removed position, complaining that neither "the enemy nor any one else '*will ever find us*.'" Combat was more than just a place where one army could demonstrate its superiority over the other; it was also an arena where youths could prove their manhood, where individuals could pass the test of courage in front of their peers. Under the enormous stress of battle, soldiers learned whether they and their friends could be counted on in moments of crisis or whether they were untrustworthy and unreliable.[42]

For most men, the reality of combat was a rude awakening. "It was hell—there's no doubt of that," insisted a Massachusetts man, "or at least about as good an imitation as is often produced in the upper world and I doubt if Satan himself could have improved upon it much." A Confederate soldier concurred: "I have heard talk of war & read of war but never could I realise its horrors until I experienced it. I have been in 4 fights in one week & marched all the time, have seen thousands of dead men & horses, and even the Woods cut to peaces by the heavy Artilery. I feel more humble & thank ful to Almighty God than ever before, thus far he has let better men fall & spared me, which Only God could do, as the amount of Lead and Iron that rained about me it seamed meracilous that I was saved."[43]

A private in a New Jersey battery admitted, "The first time that bullets whistled past my ears I confess that my heart fluttered, but 10 minutes afterward I did not seem to care anything about them nor for shot and shell that buzzed past us." He also learned in his first fight that "a *miss* is as good as if it were a mile off." Eventually, many accustomed themselves to battle, kept their wits, and simply performed their duty. Others, however, constantly battled fright, particularly before engaging the enemy. A Connecticut infantryman recalled, "I never could rid myself of a sneaking desire to turn and run for all I was worth, but I wouldn't have run for a good deal more than I was worth." A Confederate wrote home that he and a number of comrades suffered from diarrhea before battle: "I had quite a great fear that something disgraceful might happen and it was uppermost in my mind; but to my surprise the excitement or something else, had effected a cure."[44]

The battlefield dictated its own set of standards very different from those of the peacetime world. For some, combat reaffirmed these men's previous belief in themselves and their comrades. But performance in battle also elevated nobodies to greatness and demoted prominent individuals to insignificance. According to one Yankee, "Many were mere boys, many men of scant education; many were thought to be men of small soul and to fill places in civil life with little credit. Yet one could not fail to note the wondrous changes wrought in the lives and characters of some of these patriots." In civilian pursuits the lives of some soldiers were mundane and their accomplishments minor, yet with a uniform on their back and a weapon in hand they blossomed. Like Ulysses S. Grant, they somehow managed to excel in combat. For some it was the structure of military life, while others drew strength from the unique opportunity the war offered to size themselves up against their peers. Regardless, the military experience provided these men with a new self-confidence.[45]

Yet combat was a horrifying ordeal in which tens of thousands of young men lost their lives and countless more suffered physical and emotional injuries. Because of its costs, those who had been through it learned much about life and themselves and cherished the lessons. Henry Crydenwise, a New York sergeant, compared his battlefield education favorably to his three years in college: "Ah! the lessons or experience one gets from one battlefield is of no mean worth and one which can be acquired in no other place." He had faced and coped with death and had demonstrated his ability to perform his duties under the greatest duress. With death all around him, Crydenwise had an enhanced respect for his friends, teachers, and school. In a sense, he had a renewed admiration and yearning for everything that he had taken for granted before the war, and it kept him going in the most brutal moments and offered him something for which to live.[46]

Soldiers on both sides endured brushes with death. At Shiloh in April 1862, one man had a ball strike his cartridge box, buckshot pass through his hat, and grapeshot strike his neck, but he somehow survived. In the Seven Days' battles in the summer of 1862, Confederates riddled a Yankee: "Three guns, one after another, were shot to pieces in my hands, and one of these was struck twice before I threw it away. My canteen was shot through, and I was struck in three places by balls, one over the left eye, one in the left shoulder, and one in the left leg, and the deepest wound was not over half an inch, and I came off the field unhurt." A musket ball struck one black soldier in the head, skimmed around his skull without penetrating it, and exited on the opposite side. After the fight, his comrades insisted that the ball "sang out 'too thick' and passed on."[47]

One of the most humorous but at the same time dangerous incidents involved Illinois Sergeant William Parkinson at the battle of Fort Donelson in February 1862. Parkinson was at the head of his company in the front rank and lay down on his stomach to load and fire. A comrade named Sim Copple managed to lie about five feet behind the line, directly behind Parkinson. When Parkinson lifted his head to fire at the enemy, "Sim blazed away, & I thought in my sole my head was bursted wide open, I jumped up on my knees & said God Almighty dam you, come into the ranks & fight. I then called McKee & told him if he did not keep them damd boys in the ranks, I would get out of their way, for I would not stand two fires."[48]

Others were not so fortunate. Large rounds and exploding shells created ghastly wounds, and shattered limbs or lacerated arteries required amputation for survival. One soldier wrote of Gettysburg, "The sights and smells that assailed us were simply indescribably— corpses swollen to twice their original size, some of them actually burst asunder with the pressure of foul gases and vapors. . . . The odors were nauseating and so deadly that in a short time we all sickened and were lying with our mouths close to the ground, most of us vomiting profusely." After the Seven Days' battles, a horrified Confederate reported to his wife, "The air is putrid with decaying bodies of men & horses. My God, My God, what a scourge is war."[49]

Two hundred thousand young men, in the prime of health, fell in battle, and perhaps 500,000 more were injured or maimed. Each was someone's son, someone's husband, someone's brother, someone's friend. Most were individuals who had yet to make their mark on the world. No one can estimate the toll their loss exacted from society.

Families dangled in trepidation for the casualty lists after major battles. The wait seemed interminable, only to be repeated after the next engagement. Finally, word arrived: a son, husband, or brother was among the killed. Usually he was buried on the field, in a grave with only a wooden board or a crude cross. Sometimes haste did not permit even this simple rite. A friend or an officer would secure the dead man's possessions and send them home at the first opportunity. Among those who lost loved ones in the war, the Montgomery family of Mississippi considered themselves fortunate. Their dying son dictated some final words on stationery stained with his blood.

Dear Father—

This is my last letter to you. I went into battle this evening as courier for General Heth. I have been struck by a piece of shell and my right shoulder is horribly mangled and I know death is inevitable. I am very weak but I write to you because I know you would be delighted to read a word from your dying son. I know death is near, that I will die far from home and friends of my early youth but I have friends here too who are kind to me. My friend Fairfax will write you at my request and give you the particulars of my death. My grave will be marked 58 that you may visit it if you desire to do so, but it is optionary with you whether you let my remains rest here or in Miss. I would like to rest in the grave yard with my dear mother and brothers but it's a matter of minor importance. Let us all try to reunite in heaven. I pray my God to forgive my sins and I feel that his promises are true that he will forgive me and save me. Give my love to all my friends my strength fails me. My horse and my equipments will be left for you. Again a long farewell to you. May we meet in heaven.

Your dying son,
J. R. Montgomery[50]

All the hardships, losses, and sacrifices challenged these soldiers of democracy to justify the war and reexamine their commitment. They could not merely accept their government's argument. The soldiers were individualistic, accustomed to formulating their own opinions and controlling their own destinies. Some mulled over the situation and concluded that the cost of independence or reunion was too high. These men deserted their cause or counted the days until their term of service expired, all the while seeking safe duty well to the rear. Others emerged from the exploratory process with renewed support for their cause.

Once southerners endorsed secession, no great political issues initiated a widespread debate on the war and its cost until the conflict was already lost. Instead, political divisions splintered the war effort at home, while military resources dwindled at the front. A Confederate presidential election in 1864 might have forced a full and open discussion and resulted in a consensus on the war and a strengthened commitment to see it through to victory, regardless of the price. Without such a referendum, critics harped on administration policies, belittled personalities, and eventually undercut wartime unity. In early 1865, the Confederacy took up the subject of black military service, an issue that struck at the core of the entire rebellion. With the enormous weight of Robert E. Lee behind the measure, the Confederate Congress narrowly authorized the policy, but it was ineffective.

For Federals, the process was more painful, but the results of the debate strengthened public support and invigorated the war effort. Two major events, the Emancipation Proclamation in September 1862 and the presidential election of 1864, caused both soldiers and civilians to reexamine their motives and assess the progress of the war. The Emancipation Proclamation divided northerners initially, but in the long run it dramatically strengthened efforts at reunion. Abolitionists in uniform no longer wrestled with the uncomfortable position of defending a constitution that shielded slavery; soldiers realized that the Lincoln administration would adopt an extremely controversial policy and draw on any resource, including blacks, to support soldiers in the field; and the decision to set the Union on a course to extinguish slavery ultimately led to nearly 180,000 blacks taking up arms to restore the Union and to help destroy slavery.

The 1864 election forced northerners in and out of military to reconsider their support and evaluate Lincoln's direction of the war effort. Troops read newspapers voraciously, attended lectures, corresponded with loved ones, and thrashed out viewpoints around campfires. In their minds, the election was a referendum on the war. "This Day will Deside weather the Union will be Saved or Distroyed," a corporal recorded on November 8. In the end, Lincoln won a resounding endorsement. Four of every five soldiers who voted cast their ballots for the president. These troops, moreover, were Lincoln's most effective political campaigners. "Now, Father," counseled an Illinois veteran, "do not, if you love your Country, your God and your children, have anything to do with destroying this glorious Union, which your Sons have, and are, periling their lives to protect. Shun all disloyal company and do not vote the copperhead ticket, no matter who may say it is right." An Ohioan bluntly told his sister, "Tell Ben if he votes for Mc[Clellan] I will never speak to him again."[51]

Rather than dividing the public and the army, the evaluation process united Federal forces and enhanced their resolve to see the war through to a conclusion. Union troops began to perceive the Southern nation, its soldiers, and its civilians as the enemy and regarded anything that contributed to the Rebel war effort as a legitimate military target. With the raiding strategy of Grant and Sherman, Federals launched campaigns to consume Confederate foodstuffs, destroy rail lines and industry, confiscate slaves, and terrify the populace. Such operations diminished resources for Confederate armies and compelled Rebel soldiers to choose between the welfare of their families and the survival of their government. They had enlisted to protect their right to own and employ slaves and to defend hearth and home; the raiding strategy demonstrated that Confederates had accomplished neither objective.

As Union commands roared through southern regions, exposing how weak the defenders had become, Confederate soldiers lost faith in their cause. "Our soldiers are very much dishartened and the most of them say we are whiped," wrote a disconsolate Alabama private. "Our affairs are, apparently, hopeless," admitted a South Carolinian after the fall of Savannah. "Nothing but Divine interposition can save us from subjugation." Confederates deserted to look after their families, thereby reducing troop strength and enabling Union forces to penetrate deeper into the interior. More Southern lives were disrupted, and more Rebel troops deserted. Union armies trapped the Confederacy in a spiral of defeat.[52]

Few anticipated the speed of Confederate collapse. Outflanked in late March 1865, Lee's army surrendered at Appomattox Courthouse in April, and the bottom quickly fell out of the Southern war effort. Over the next few weeks, the remaining secessionist armies yielded to Federal forces. An exhausted Confederacy had nothing left. The war was over.

For the victors, there were parades and celebrations. Huge crowds came out to see the two primary field commands march through the streets of Washington, D.C. Other soldiers received raucous receptions from friends and family. The men in gray simply walked home.

Despite uttering platitudes about reuniting the nation, soldiers were unenthusiastic about reconciliation. After some difficult years, Confederate veterans cast aside Federal designs for a reconstructed South and restored themselves to power over blacks. In the North, politicians waved the "bloody shirt" for the next two decades to remind voters just who had stepped forward in the fight to preserve the Union.

With time, though, some deep wounds healed. Late in life, men on both sides pushed aside old grudges and joined hands at several major battlefields to commemorate those momentous events. Gone was youth. Gone was intense hostility. Gone were many comrades who had fought there. All that was left were fading memories. At one time in the soldiers' lives, as Oliver Wendell Holmes said, they had been touched by fire. They had rushed to arms and endured unforeseen hardships and consequences. Passions now had dissipated, and all that was left was a perception about war. In the midst of that struggle, an Illinois surgeon recorded a few words that reflected the sentiments of many veterans. "There is no God in war," he wrote in late 1864. "It is merciless, cruel, vindictive, un-christian, savage, relentless. It is all that devils could wish for."[53]

Notes

1. Quoted in Joseph T. Glatthaar, *Forged in Battle: The Civil War Alliance of Black Soldiers and White Officers* (New York: Free Press, 1990), 26–27; P. T. Vaughn to Ginnie, October 11, 1864, in Alice V. D. Pierrepont, *Reuben Vaughn Kidd: Soldier of the Confederacy* (Petersburg, Va.: n.p., 1947), 358.

2. Quoted in James M. McPherson, *Battle Cry of Freedom: The Civil War Era* (New York: Oxford University Press, 1988), 241, 244.

3. Quoted in James M. McPherson, *What They Fought For, 1861–1865* (Baton Rouge: Louisiana State University Press, 1994), 48.

4. W. P. Heflin, *Blind Man "on the Warpath"* (n.p., 1900?), 69.

5. Randall C. Jimerson, *The Private Civil War: Popular Thought during the Sectional Crisis* (Baton Rouge: Louisiana State University Press, 1988), 18.

6. Jno. Winfield to wife, September 2, 1861, John J. Winfield Papers, Southern Historical Collection, University of North Carolina at Chapel Hill; Will [Crutcher] to "Darling," October 26, 1861, Crutcher-Shannon Papers, Barker Texas History Center, Austin.

7. Quoted in Jimerson, *Private Civil War*, 24; Thomas J. Owen to Sallie, November 12, 1861, Thomas J. Owen Papers, Georgia Department of Archives and History, Atlanta (hereafter cited as GADAH).

8. Quoted in McPherson, *What They Fought For*, 30.

9. Quoted ibid., 32.

10. Quoted in Bell I. Wiley, *The Life of Billy Yank: The Common Soldier of the Civil War* (Baton Rouge: Louisiana State University Press, 1978), 41; SMQ to mother, July 31, 1861, Quincy, Wendell, Holmes, and Upham Families Papers, Massachusetts Historical Society, Boston.

11. John A. Wilder, "Will the American Experiment Fail?" unpublished commencement address at Union College, July 23, 1856, Loomis-Wilder Family Papers, Yale University, New Haven, Conn.; Joseph J. Scroggs diary, January 1, 1861, Civil War Times Illustrated Collection, U.S. Army Military History Institute, Carlisle Barracks, Pa.

12. Quoted in Jimerson, *Private Civil War*, 35.

13. Quoted in Wiley, *Life of Billy Yank*, 21; James T. Thompson to mother and sisters, August 12, 1861, in Aurelia Austin, ed., "A Georgia Boy with 'Stonewall' Jackson," *Virginia Magazine of History and Biography* 70 (July 1962): 316–17.

14. Bell I. Wiley, *The Life of Johnny Reb: The Common Soldier of the Confederacy* (Baton Rouge: Louisiana State University Press, 1978), 20.

15. Jno. M. Tilley to wife, July 18, 1861, John M. Tilley Papers, GADAH.

16. Letter to the editors of the *Enquirer,* December 30, 1863, W. S. Morris Papers, Museum of the Confederacy, Richmond, Va. (hereafter cited as MC).

17. P. G. Harrison to friend, October 13, [?], Cabell Family Papers, University of Virginia, Charlottesville.

18. Thomas F. Green to Matty, March 6, 1863, Thomas Fitzgerald Green Civil War Letter, GADAH. See Joseph T. Glatthaar, *The March to the Sea and Beyond: Sherman's Troops in the Savannah and Carolinas Campaigns* (New York: New York University Press, 1985), 107; and Compiled Military Service Record of Nelson B. Bartram, B, 17th New York Infantry, RG 94, National Archives.

19. John O'Farrell diary, March 1, 1863, John O'Farrell Papers, MC.

20. Quoted in James I. Robertson, Jr., *Soldiers Blue and Gray* (Columbia: University of South Carolina Press, 1988), 20–21.

21. Charles H. Spencer to mother, May 11, 1865, Charles H. Spencer Papers, State Historical Society of Wisconsin, Madison.

22. Glatthaar, *March*, 107–8; Wm. H. Ker to sister, May 10, 1863, William H. Ker Papers, Louisiana State University, Baton Rouge.

23. Heflin, *Blind Man*, 18.

24. D. S. Freeman, *R. E. Lee: A Biography* (New York: Scribner's, 1935–36), 2:496–97; George Clark, *A Glance Backward, or Some Events in the Past History of My Life* (Houston: Press of Rein and Sons, 1914?), 45–46.

25. Wiley, *Life of Johnny Reb*, 52.

26. Quoted in Glatthaar, *March*, 75.

27. Chas. S. Brown to mother, Etta, Lew, Fred, and all the rest, January 15, 1865, Charles S. Brown Papers, Duke University, Durham, N.C.; George Baird diary, December 18, 1864, in Alonzo L. Brown, *History of the Fourth Regiment of Minnesota Infantry Volunteers* (St. Paul: Pioneer Press, 1892), 350–51; William B. Miller diary, January 5, 1865, William B. Miller Papers, Indiana Historical Society, Indianapolis.

28. Josiah B. Patterson to wife, December 4, 1861, Josiah Blair Patterson Papers, GADAH; Wyman Folsom to mother, October 30, 1863, Folsom Family Papers, Minnesota Historical Society, St. Paul; Charlie to Katie, April 2, 1865, in Lorna Lutes Sylvester, ed., "'Gone for a Soldier': The Civil War Letters of Charles Harding Cox," *Indiana Magazine of History* 68 (September 1972): 233.

29. Bob Douglass to sister, September 10, 1864, Robert O. Douglass Papers, GADAH.

30. James W. Wright to parents, April 24, 1864, John Wright Family Papers, North Carolina Division of Archives and History, Raleigh; John T. Smith to mother and sisters, February 1, 1863, Smith-Johnson Papers, MC.

31. Quoted in Glatthaar, *Forged*, 20.

32. T. C. Brady to wife and son, January 13, 1865, quoted in Glatthaar, *March*, 104.

33. James T. Thompson to [family], October 5, 1862, in Austin, ed., "Georgia Boy," 331; Halsey Wigfall to Louly, July 18, 1863, Louis T. Wigfall Papers, Library of Congress; Robert E. Park diary, September 11, 1864, in *Southern Historical Society Papers*, 1:435.

34. William Fisher Plane to [wife], September 5, 1862, quoted in Glatthaar, *March*, 115.

35. Quoted ibid.

36. Wiley, *Life of Johnny Reb*, 248.

37. James Rogers to ?, April 18, 1863, James Rogers Papers, Sophia Smith Collection, Smith College, Northampton, Mass.

38. Leonard G. Phenix to editor, February 21, 1865, *Christian Recorder*, March 25, 1865; H. H. Hood to wife, May 22, 1865, H. H. Hood Papers, Illinois State Historical Library, Springfield.

39. H. H. Hood to wife, November 24, 1862, H. H. Hood Papers.

40. Glatthaar, *Forged*, 20; Glatthaar, *March*, 109.

41. Quoted in Glatthaar, *Forged*, 20–21; Taylor Scott to Fan, March 29, 1862, Keith Family Papers, Virginia Historical Society, Richmond; Joe D. Shields to father, July 1, 1861, Joseph D. Shields Papers, Louisiana State University.

42. Anonymous, "A Sketch of Twelve Months Service in the Mobile Rifle Company," *Alabama Historical Quarterly* 25 (Spring–Summer 1963): 156.

43. Quoted in Glatthaar, *Forged*, 21; J. A. Gillespie to wife, July 5, 1862, Jaspar A. Gillespie Papers, GADAH.

44. Quoted in Glatthaar, *Forged*, 21; Wiley, *Life of Johnny Reb*, 31–32.

45. A. W. Greely, *Reminiscences of Adventure and Service* (New York: Scribner's, 1927), 88. See also James Horrocks to parents, January 9, 186[5], in Horrocks, *My Dear Parents: The Civil War Seen by an English Union Sol-*

dier, ed. A. S. Lewis (San Diego: Harcourt Brace Jovanovich, 1982), 115; W. Goodale to children, May 7, 1865, Warren Goodale Papers, Massachusetts Historical Society; Sam Evans to father, May 1, 1862, Evans Family Papers, Thomas Hopes to sister, September 23, 1862, Thomas Hopes Papers, both at Ohio Historical Society, Columbus.

46. Henry Crydenwise to family, July 6, 1863, Henry M. Crydenwise Papers, Emory University, Atlanta.

47. Glatthaar, *Forged,* 23, 161.

48. William Parkinson to [Sarah?], April 15, 1862, William H. Parkinson Papers, Emory University.

49. Wiley, *Life of Johnny Reb,* 75; William Fisher Plane to wife, July 8, 1862, in S. Joseph Lewis, Jr., ed., "Letters of William Fisher Plane, C.S.A., to His Wife," *Georgia Historical Quarterly* 48 (June 1964): 223.

50. J. R. Montgomery to father, [June] 1864, James R. Montgomery Papers, MC.

51. Glatthaar, *March,* 47, 49.

52. John Cotton to wife, January 20, 1865, in Lucille Griffith, ed., *Yours till Death: Civil War Letters of W. Cotton* (University, Ala.: University of Alabama Press, 1951), 125; Robert Gourdin to sister, December 26, 1864, Gourdin-Young Papers, Emory University.

53. Quoted in Glatthaar, *March,* 174.

Freedmen in Richmond, Virginia. A black family and a group of men are seated along the canal with ruins in the background. Courtesy Library of Congress.

Mirrors beyond Memories:
Afro-Virginians and the Civil War

Ervin L. Jordan, Jr.

DURING THE CIVIL WAR centennial I was an elementary school student in an all-black Norfolk, Virginia, housing project. One day, while in the school library, I discovered a fascinating book written in plain language and filled with photographs and colorful maps—*The American Heritage Picture History of the Civil War*. While browsing its pages, I noticed photographs of black soldiers, including Major Martin R. Delany, one of the Union army's first black commissioned officers. I remember experiencing astonishment because my teachers had never mentioned the existence of black soldiers. Unquestionably, there were serious gaps in the history of the war regarding African Americans.[1]

I decided to become a historian and write a book about the active roles of blacks in Civil War Virginia. Three decades later and after six years of formal research, I wrote *Black Confederates and Afro-Yankees in Civil War Virginia*, from which the examples in this essay are taken.

IN SPRING 1991, the Virginia state flag flew at half mast over the remains of an unknown Confederate soldier lying in state at the capitol. The body, discovered by relic hunters in Chesterfield County who anonymously turned it over to authorities with a request for burial in a Confederate cemetery, lay in its Stars and Bars–draped flat pine coffin at the foot of a statue of Robert E. Lee and surrounded by an honor guard consisting of Sons of Confederate Veterans dressed in Confederate uniforms. Virginia Governor L. Douglas Wilder, grandson of slaves and America's first elected black governor, and African-American civil rights groups did not oppose the ceremony. Several Afro-Virginians also paid their respects. The president of the state chapter of the Southern Christian Leadership Conference expressed conciliation: "He can't do us harm now."[2]

However, most contemporary Americans seem embarrassed, indifferent, or defensive about the legacy of slavery and believe the less said of it the better. Many African Americans have apparently concluded that between the end of slavery and the beginning of the modern civil rights movement little in black history is worthy of acclaim; both races behave as if there is a stigma of silence to be imposed on consideration of certain aspects of America's racial past. But we can learn so much from and about each other, and we must honestly face our history to transcend it. Until African-American voices were heard more clearly in the late twentieth century, stereotypical orthodoxy about their lives in the South was unchallenged. They were the forgotten participants of the Civil War, thanks to the ritual reconciliation between North and South. Most Americans accepted the South's claim that the war was caused by obscure constitutional issues such as state's rights, not by slavery. The struggles and sacrifices of African-American soldiers and civilians and the history of slavery were excluded, distorted, and ignored.

The African-American experience continues to suffer from cultural amnesia. Civil War blacks, with a few exceptions, are barely commemorated by historical markers. In Alexandria, Virginia, the site of Price, Birch, and Company, one of the South's most infamous slave-trading offices, has been designated a national landmark: victims and their oppressors both are canonized in the same place.[3] After 130 years, stereotyped representations of the roles and participation of African Americans linger; the war has become the same old story that hasn't been told. For example, entries about African Americans in a 1986 illustrated encyclopedia of the Civil War comprised less than one of the book's 849 pages, and the volume lacked biographical entries for Frederick Douglass, the most influential African American of the nineteenth century, Harriet Tubman, and William Carney, the first black soldier to win the Congressional Medal of Honor. During the past thirty years, history has become a means for the empowerment and recognition of the achievements of groups previously overlooked. In this sense the (recent) writing of American history has largely become the recovery of memory. Nowhere is this more true that in the extraordinary growth and development of African-American studies.[4]

Slavery and Freedom

Of the Confederacy's 3.5 million blacks, 550,000 resided in Virginia; one in six Confederate blacks were Afro-Virginians. More African Americans lived in Virginia than anywhere else in North America; according to the 1860 census, 490,000 slaves and 59,000 free blacks resided in the Old Dominion. Of Virginia's 1.6 million inhabitants, 35 percent were black. Of 148 counties, sixty-two (41 percent) were predominantly black, and in forty-four counties Afro-Virginians were the majority, ranging as high as 74 percent of the population. In many regards, Virginia was a biracial commonwealth.

The typical Afro-Virginian was a slave, and slave trading was extensive in most of the state. At birth each slave was allegedly worth about $300; one Confederate periodical unpersuasively called breeding an accident of the southern climate's stimulating effects yet in the same breath candidly admitted that Alabama, Louisiana, and Mississippi bred slaves for interstate commerce. Alexandria was one of Virginia's main slave-trading centers. Franklin and Armfield's slave pens remained in business until the Union seized the town in May 1861. This well-run establishment, founded in 1828, clothed its slaves before putting them on display and usually shipped up to a hundred at a time to New Orleans chained in pairs with armed guards.

Alexandria was also home to Kephart and Company, "the chief slave dealing firm in the State." After the town's capture this firm's building was converted into a jail for Confederate prisoners of war. Between Payne and West Streets was the Duke Street firm of Price, Birch, and Company, "Dealers in Slaves." Its earthen floors, windowless cells, iron bar doors and manacles made it a serviceable place to house slaves and, later, insubordinate Union soldiers.[5]

Richmond trading firms such as Silas and R. H. Omohundro saw increasing profits although their merchandise's availability became uncertain as the war continued. As of 1863–64 Omohundro's quarterly sales totaled $13,000; during July 1864 the sale of four slaves alone netted $18,550, of which the Omohundros earned a commission of $1,392.[6]

At the beginning of the war, slaves were given misinformation and told that Northerners were coming south to kill and eat them, to use their bodies as fertilizer, or to sell them in Haiti or Cuba as slaves. Yankees had four legs, one eye in front of and one eye behind the head, and horns on top. These untruths were believed by some slaves, and Union soldiers reported that blacks fled from them in terror. But most were not deceived by Confederate propaganda: "Masters have tried to make us believe that the Yankees only wished to sell us to Cuba, to get money to carry on the war," a congregation of escaped slaves told a Northern clergyman in September 1861.[7]

Slaves did not dally passively singing spirituals while awaiting deliverance by the Union army: the number of slaves who fled Virginia increased steadily. Of 472,528 slaves in 1850, eighty-three officially escaped (one of every 5,693); of 490,865 slaves in 1860, 117 ran away (one of every 4,195). By 1863, 37,706 slaves out of a population of 346,848 (one of every nine, or 11 percent) successfully escaped in spite of slave patrols and the presence of heavily armed Confederate troops and state militia, and this figure does not include unreported escapes. Runaways escaped from prominent Confederate slaveholders. After Jim Turner, body servant of former governor Henry A. Wise, escaped during the Union capture of Norfolk in 1862, Wise angrily declared that all runaway slaves should be shot on sight. Years later, Turner reappeared—at Wise's funeral. Fluvanna County slave James Woodson fled his brutal master and joined Sheridan's cavalry during its Virginia raids. His son, born in 1875 in Buckingham County, was Carter G. Woodson, later known as the father of African-American History.[8]

While many Afro-Virginians fled alone or even in groups of thirty or forty, some returned with Union soldiers to pillage farms, rescue family members, or establish bases for armed guerrilla warfare. Slaveowners in isolated areas and in territories controlled by the Union were especially targeted. These part-time guerrillas established colonies near cities and towns, and whites who ventured beyond urban areas dared do so only in heavily armed groups. A September 1861 newspaper editorial warned that black underground camps would increase to menacing magnitudes unless destroyed. Afro-Virginian "land pirates" even attacked McClellan's Army of the Potomac as it moved through Virginia in 1862. In March 1864, five hundred black men in Mathews County engaged in raids that shattered slaveowners' domination, and a fifty-four-year-old former slave named Bill was described as the "master of the land."[9]

Free blacks were perhaps the war's most invisible people. Approximately 251,000 of them resided in the slaveholding South in 1860, and 59,000 of them lived in Virginia—more than in any other slave state except Maryland. Free blacks were vulnerable to harsh ordinances and suspected of being runaway slaves. By law they were forbidden to practice specific occupations or to sell agricultural products without a license, but many could and did earn a humble livelihood. Proud of their free status, they considered themselves the black aristocracy of the state, and they proudly boasted after 1865 that they had not been "shot free."

Some whites grudgingly respected free blacks by conceding a need for their labor. Residents in Isle of Wight and Nansemond Counties strongly opposed government proposals to banish free blacks from those areas because they comprised an indispensable cheap labor caste. Rockbridge County residents petitioned their court in October 1863 for the return of Washington Jackson, a forty-eight-year-old free Afro-Virginian blacksmith conscripted for Confederate military work. "A very industrious man," Jackson had resided in the county since 1840 and owned real and personal property assessed at more than $1,700. One resident testified, "I do not know how the farming community can get along if he is Taken from us."[10]

Religion

In 1861 approximately 417,000 Afro-Christians lived in the South. Slaves believed that they were God's chosen people and that he had promised to set them free. This hope originated from the similar experiences of biblical Hebrews held in bondage in Egypt. A slave named Aunt Aggy stated, "I allers knowed [freedom] was a-comin. I allers heerd de rumblin' o' de wheels. I allers 'spected to see white folks heaped up dead. An' de Lor', He's kept His promise, an' 'venged His people, jes' as I knowed He would." [11]

Many slaves were willing disciples of Christianity, but just as many probably scorned the racist hypocrisy practiced by slaveowners. One Virginia slave woman recalled, "My mistress was a dreadful pious woman. She would pray, ever so long in the morning, then come out and sit in her rocking chair, with her cowhide [whip] and cut and slash everybody who passed her. . . . Sometimes I was afraid she was not a Christian, but she was mighty pious." An indignant Fauquier County slave husband refused his wife's entreaty that he join her church: "How can Jesus be just, if He will allow such oppression and wrong? Don't the slaveholders justify their conduct by the Bible itself, and say that it tells them to do so? How can God be just, when He not only permits, but sanctions such conduct?"[12]

Christianity paradoxically urged resistance to oppression in the Old Testament but urged acceptance of one's fate and obedience to authority in the New Testament. Religion provided godly comfort, emotional release, group identification, the covert development of a black intelligentsia (preachers, ministers, deacons), and a sense of community against an antagonistic white society. Slaves understood that religion was employed by whites as a tool for controlling them. Nonetheless, they retained or rejected those parts of Christianity they deemed false in favor of an Afro-Christianity that promised deliverance from earthly slavery.

Christianity did not eliminate supernaturalism among blacks or whites. Upon hearing the distant rumble of a thunderstorm, one Fauquier County slaveholder would nervously order twenty of his slaves to his room to stand in a circle while he sat in their midst. He presumed that God would not strike slaves with lightning and believed their nearness would protect him. Other slaves allegedly caused poltergeistic occurrences: furniture and various household objects were flung about by invisible forces only when certain slaves were present. Astral projections of a Bath County slave named Millie in 1863 were omens of death and ill fortune for Orrick family. So frightening were these sightings that Millie's mistress forced her to sleep alone in a room locked from the outside, but a doppelganger of the slave woman continued to walk through the walls of the house, to the utter terror of the Orricks.[13]

Crimes and Punishments

There were five crimes that, if inflicted by blacks upon whites, would result in punishment, including fines, whippings, imprisonment, enslavement, and even death: murder or striking a white person, arson, running away, stealing, and impertinent language. If guilty of conspiring to kill or injure a white person, the penalty was death or ten years' confinement for a free black; a slave could be executed or sold outside Virginia. Floggings were permitted for insolence, threatening gestures, providing passes to slaves without their owner's permission, firearms possession, taking part in riots, subversive utterances and publications, and selling or administering medicines without a white person's explicit permission. Blacks accused of felonies were entitled to legal representation, trial by jury, and the right of appeal. During 1861–64 eighty Afro-Virginian slave convicts, with a combined value of $97,000, were shipped to the Deep South.[14]

According to Booker T. Washington, whites most frequently accused blacks of stealing, and he complained that Afro-Americans were unjustly accused of being dishonest. Washington recalled how his mother constantly stole food for her children, and he acknowledged that by certain ethical standards her actions were unscrupulous. But such acts were necessary for slaves to survive.[15]

The must frequent method of punishment was the whip. Austin Steward, a Virginia slave, described one whip as nine feet long, made of tough cowhide, and having a butt end weighted with lead. Several commentators mentioned how terribly slaves' backs were scarred. The customary medical treatment consisted of animal fat or "Negro plaster," a rubbing compound of witch hazel, mustard, pepper, salt, and vinegar that healed without scarring (to conceal a troublemaker from potential buyers), but many slaves swore some remedies hurt worse than the floggings.

A variety of grotesque code words described whippings: "teasings"; "to hug the post"; "to kiss the cowhide"; "strap-hopping"; "negro desserts"; "leather-lessons"; or "ticklings." Confederates used these terms to avoid offending the British and French, from whom the South wanted diplomatic recognition, and to portray slave brutality incidents as distorted by the Northern abolitionist news media. State law forbade more than thirty-nine lashes, but dosages of five hundred were routine. Victims were tied to posts, staked out naked on the ground, stretched across barrels, or dangled from trees to receive the utmost force of lashes. Some professional slave whippers spread straw around the whipping site to prevent blood from soaking their shoes.[16]

Slaves occasionally wreaked vengeance on owners who whipped them. William H. Clopton was a Charles City County slaveowner and Confederate sympathizer known as his county's most disreputable slaveholder. He was fond of whipping nude slave women. In May 1864 Clopton was captured by troops under the command of Union General Edward Augustus Wild, an abolitionist and recruiter of black soldiers. He presented whips to the slaves and told them to take their revenge. Clopton was tied to a tree in front of the general's headquarters, stripped, and lashed by three of his former female victims.[17]

Rebellion and Emancipation

Some historians have suggested that wartime slaves failed to revolt merely because they did not think of it; others believe that African Americans viewed the conflict as a white man's war and were content to remain on the sidelines. Slaves realized the quarreling whites of the North and South would quickly put aside their differences long enough to crush any black revolt. In March 1861 forty Northumberland County slaves were arrested for attempted poisoning. Much to the consternation of whites, the blacks had decided that Lincoln's inauguration made them free men and decided to kill their masters before leaving the county. In Culpeper County in 1863, a black conspiracy caused whites "the greatest consternation imaginable." After copies of Northern newspapers containing the text of Lincoln's preliminary Emancipation Proclamation were found in their possession, seventeen blacks, mostly free, were hanged.[18]

It is possible that General Robert E. Lee, commander of the Army of Northern Virginia, personally freed more slaves than President Lincoln. Three days before the Emancipation Proclamation went into effect, Lee complied with the provisions of the antebellum will of his deceased father-in-law, George Washington Parke Custis (who died in 1857), and as his legal executor freed 194 slaves. Custis's will had directed that his slaves be emancipated within five years of his death. Lee ignored this awkward wartime coincidence and appeared before a Spotsylvania County justice of the peace on December 29, 1862, to transform thirty slave groups into free black families.[19]

The only Afro-Virginians who could publicly celebrate the Emancipation Proclamation were in the areas it exempted, such as Norfolk, scene of the largest Afro-Virginian public commemoration of the proclamation. Four thousand blacks paraded through the city streets; in one wagon a group of black women gleefully tore up Confederate flags. The festivities concluded with a burning in effigy of Jefferson Davis.[20]

Davis retaliated by issuing a broadside reply, "An Address to the People of the Free States by the President of the Southern Confederacy," on January 5, 1863. He blamed abolitionists for the Union's enlistment of black soldiers and proclaimed that all free blacks and their descendants, both in the Confederacy and seized in territories captured by Confederate forces, would become slaves as of February 22, 1863. With the exceptions of incidents like those that occurred during the Gettysburg campaign (during which Confederate soldiers seized free blacks and shipped them back to Virginia for sale) the Davis proclamation seems to have never been seriously enforced by Confederate authorities.[21]

Women

Slave women are generally characterized by historians as docile, but many participated in acts of resistance. Family heirlooms were among the casualties in the guerrilla wars black women waged against their female oppressors. A Norfolk County slave named Mahala deliberately broke the finest French china of her mistress whenever disagreements arose on their isolated farm. Assaults on white men by Afro-Virginian women were not unusual. Columbia Anderson, a dishwasher at the Georgia House Hotel in Richmond, was described in 1862 as a "known [white] man-beater" whenever she became intoxicated.[22]

Rape is the silent subject of the Civil War; it is alluded to in letters, memoirs, and reports in a cloud of euphemisms created by tight-lipped Victorian prudes. In April 1862, B. E. Harrison of Prince William County was appalled by the rape of one of his slaves as a squad of Federal soldiers plundered his home. Four white Union cavalrymen raped two Newport News free black women during the last week of July 1862. However, some white Union soldiers paid for their lust with their lives. Black vigilantes killed a white sailor in 1863 after his attempted rape of a black girl in Yorktown.

Confederates also committed rape. In July 1862 Dillard McCormick, a member of the Richmond police force, was indicted for the rape of Ann Eliza Wells. Although the crime was witnessed by fellow officers, McCormick was acquitted but dismissed from the police force.

Archibald Wilkinson, a Confederate marine, was arrested for raping Margaret Willis, a free black Richmond woman, during November 1862.[23]

Black women were also the victims of forced breeding. In the spring 1862, Union soldiers temporarily occupied an estate near the Pamunkey River whose remaining slave women, children, and old men (the able-bodied males all having fled or been taken to the interior by their owner) were of "all colors." Inquisitive but suspecting the truth, the soldiers questioned the white overseer about the profitability of slave breeding. He conceded the breeding of slaves as his plantation's chief source of income with a yearly "crop" of fifteen to twenty blacks valued at $1,200 each. When asked how the black human "crop" been delivered to market for sale, the overseer cagily replied that they were sold south and had "brought a right smart bit of money." The fertility of female slaves was among Virginia's steadiest sources of wealth.[24]

According to the 1860 census, 40 percent of Virginia's free blacks and 15 percent of its slaves were the result of miscegenation. Contrary to white refutations, miscegenation customarily involved a white man and black (slave) woman; these situations occurred more often than has been generally admitted. Henry Estabrooks, a Union officer who escaped from Richmond, was constantly startled by Afro-Virginians who appeared white. Some could pass for Confederate soldiers: "Presently a white man came in uniform. . . . I sprang up and thought I was betrayed; but he advanced and accosted me politely and pleasantly. I did not know what to make of him. . . . He was a slave. . . . I could scarcely believe it. He was a large, fine-looking man, with straight, light-colored hair, blue eyes, and a florid complexion. Accustomed as I had become to all shades of negro complexion, I was puzzled with him. There was not the least indication of negro blood about him. . . . His skin was much lighter than mine."[25]

Marriage

Southern opinion had long opposed interracial marriages, but they occurred nevertheless. Millie Rawls, a fifteen-year-old free black resident of Culpeper County, began a common-law marriage with George W. Jameson, a white man, in 1861 and raised five children. He faithfully supported Millie and their children and transferred all of his property to her in May 1863.[26]

Black men who cohabited with white women could be executed under Virginia law, which did not prevent Richard, a Richmond slave, from taking up residence with a consenting white woman named Delia Mack. They lived together as husband and wife until Delia's infuriated sister, Caroline, informed the police. Richard was convicted and received 117 lashes in early 1865. An Albemarle County black man named Jackson and his white wife rented a house from the University of Virginia and dwelled undisturbed by neighbors until the faculty chair suddenly demanded their eviction in October 1863. John P. Anderson, yet another free black man married to a white woman, placed his Fauquier County property in her name, and the couple resided together during the war and Reconstruction. These and other long-term interracial relationships reveal that such couplings flourished in Confederate Virginia in greater numbers than has been suspected.[27]

Despite those who declared blacks incapable of expressing compassionate feelings between a husband and wife, parent and child, slave couples genuinely cherished each other as best they could under the circumstances. One Madison County slave woman told a British tourist, "Selling is worse than flogging. My husband was sold six years ago. My heart has bled ever since, and is not well yet. I have been flogged many times, since he was torn from me, but my back has healed in time." Slaveowners opposed wartime appeals by reformers for the legal recognition and sanctity of slave marriages because such modifications would foster more problems than they would rectify as far as the relationship between master and slave was concerned. Clergymen believed that such recognition would regain God's grace for the Confederacy and thus its independence. Angry slaveholders worried that legalized slave marriages would endow slaves with civil rights, interfere with local customs, put the laws of marriage above those of property rights and slave ownership, and provide proof for abolitionist charges that slavery was and promoted debauchery.[28]

Married slaves sought to remain near their spouses. If this were not possible, conjugal visits were the norm. Many walked miles to visit each other, undaunted by slave patrols, slave stealers, bad roads, and weather. Laws did not recognize the legality of slave marriages, and the ceremonial "jumping the broom" was more of an illusion than reality. Because slave families could be and were frequently broken up by sales, slaves learned to cope through kinship networks that continued beyond the end of slavery. Slaves had limited latitude in the choice of spouses and established families and loving relationships; thousands had their marriages legalized upon reaching Union-held territories, while others undertook exhausting searches for long-sold children, spouses, and kinsfolk after the war.

Legal, church-sanctioned weddings were sought by slave couples who escaped to Union lines. They formally renewed their marriage vows with the words "till death do us part." One newspaper announced, "Married at Falls Church, Alexandria, Sunday evening, January 24th, 1864, by Rev. J. R. Johnson, missionary of the American Missionary Association, *Mr. Frederick Foote and Miss Margaret Carter*. Frederick has been six times sold as a slave. He has buried one wife, has six children in slavery, and now owns more than thirty acres of land. He thinks, and we think, too, that he can take care of himself and his family."[29]

Elizabeth Keckley

Perhaps the most remarkable Afro-Virginian of the war was Elizabeth Keckley, an ex-slave from Dinwiddie County and expert dressmaker whose reputation and skills provided for her family. Her owner permitted her to travel to New York to earn the $1,200 price of herself and her son, and with the help of friends she purchased their freedom in 1855. She obtained a position as the seamstress for Varina Davis (later First Lady of the Confederacy) in 1860 and eventually held the same position, besides that of best friend and confidant, to Mary Todd Lincoln. Keckley made the dress in which Jefferson Davis was allegedly disguised when he was captured in May 1865. According to Keckley, southerners had held secret meetings at Jefferson Davis's Washington residence in 1860 to devise a secession strategy before Lincoln's nomination. She described Varina Davis as having already given herself the title of "Mrs. President" of the Confederate States of America and as confidently expecting her husband to become the Confederacy's first president, defeat the North in a brief war, and make Washington the Confederate capital.

Keckley's 1868 autobiography, *Behind the Scenes, or Thirty Years a Slave and Four Years in the White House,* is an inside narrative of wartime Washington and life in the Lincoln White House; some of the most frequently quoted anecdotes about Lincoln and his family are found in these pages. Keckley published her reminiscences to raise funds on behalf of the widowed Mary Lincoln, but Mary and her eldest son, Robert, vehemently condemned the book when it appeared in 1868. Robert Lincoln was paranoid about what he believed were invasions of his family's privacy and used his influence to suppress the book, purchasing and destroying copies. He even hinted that a white man had written Keckley's autobiography, but to the end of her days Keckley maintained that she had penned her memoirs for the benefit of her friend. Her publication of private correspondence with Mary was perhaps ill advised, but what particularly upset Mary Lincoln was Keckley's revelation that Mary's agents secretly sold the late president's clothing in New York City to pay her enormous shopping debts. Although Mary angrily ended their friendship, Keckley never spoke ill of the former First Lady and continued as a dressmaker. She taught at Wilberforce University until her death in Washington, D.C., in May 1907; Keckley's estate, valued at $500, was bequeathed to the National Association for the Relief of Destitute Colored Women and Children.[30]

Afro-Confederates

Black loyalty to the Confederacy (usually to county, town, or state) has been treated as an inconvenient fact. By ignoring black Confederates, historians distort history. Approximately 25 percent of the Old Dominion's free blacks and 10 percent of its slaves supported the Confederacy. Afro-Confederate free blacks and slaves contributed funds and labor to the Southern cause as early as January 1861.[31]

Afro-Confederates risked much for their allegiance. A free black preacher in Hampton who had purchased his family's freedom and two houses took the Confederate side to protect his property and liberty. Other blacks considered it a sign of heavenly justice after the houses were destroyed by fire when Confederates evacuated and burned Hampton in the summer 1861. Another unidentified black Baptist minister, grateful to whites for allowing him to purchase his attractive daughter from lustful slaveowners, publicly offered his and his sons' services to Virginia and published a statement to this effect. Afro-Virginians condemned him, and the minister defended his actions with the excuse that he had done what he thought best for his fellow blacks. Then, as his congregation dwindled to almost nothing, he became alarmed. He tried to restore himself in the good graces of his people with more excuses and ultimately apologies, but the black community continued to ostracize him.[32]

The Confederate War Department at first declined to enlist black soldiers, but a group of New York soldiers on patrol from Newport News was attacked by Confederate cavalry accompanied by a body of armed blacks in December 1861. The Union troops killed six before retreating; their officers swore out an affidavit saying that they were attacked by blacks and complained, "If [the Rebels] fight us with Negroes, why should we not fight them with Negroes, too?. . . Let us fight the devil with fire." Two "fully armed" Afro-Confederate soldiers were seen on picket duty at the Confederate camps at Fredericksburg in 1862: a sketch of them appeared in *Harper's Weekly*.[33]

During the Federal siege of Yorktown in May 1862, one of the

Confederacy's chief sharpshooters was an Afro-Virginian in a brick chimney from which he shot Yankee pickets on the periphery of Camp Scott. When Federals called upon him to desert, the black sharpshooter disdained their appeals. Finally, a regiment fired a volley at his hiding place, killing him.[34]

During the Antietam campaign, Northern eyewitnesses reported the presence of armed blacks in the Army of Northern Virginia. A Union doctor, Lewis H. Steiner, recorded in his diary, "Most of the negroes . . . were manifestly an integral portion of the Southern Confederacy Army. . . . The fact was patent and rather interesting when considered in connection with the horror rebels express at the suggestion of black soldiers being employed for the National [Federal] defence." After the July 1863 Gettysburg battle, the *New York Herald* reported that among the rebel prisoners were seven fully armed blacks in Confederate uniforms.[35]

By early 1865, as its resistance weakened, the Confederacy began a public relations campaign to win over blacks. On March 13, the Confederate Congress enacted legislation authorizing the enlistment of 300,000 slave and free black troops between the ages of eighteen and forty-five to be organized into new military units. The owner's consent was required before a slave might enroll; amendments to this measure specified that manumission of slave-soldiers would be granted only with the consent of the state where they were stationed at the time of their discharges. To prevent any possibility of armed black rebellion, no more than 25 percent of the male slaves in any state were to be enlisted.[36]

On March 11, 1865, two days before the Confederate Congress approved the enlistment of blacks, the Jackson (Hospital) Battalion, comprising three companies of white convalescent soldiers and two companies of blacks, arrived at the Petersburg front. The unit entered combat just seven days after its organization and fought under the command of the commandant of the Virginia Military Institute Cadet Corps. On April 6, 1865, a squad of twelve Afro-Confederate soldiers building defenses along the road to Farmville was seen by white refugees. They were fully armed and under the command of white officers who identified them as "the only company of colored troops in the Confederate service." Of the 27,000 Confederates who surrendered and were paroled at Appomattox, approximately thirty were black.[37]

Most black male Virginians who served did so in the Union army. One of the most famous was Sergeant William H. Carney of the Fifty-fourth Massachusetts Volunteers, the first African American to receive the Medal of Honor. Born in Norfolk, Virginia, in 1840, Carney fled to Massachusetts and enlisted at New Bedford. During the regiment's ill-fated assault against Fort Wagner, South Carolina, on July 18, 1863 (the subject of the 1989 Academy Award–winning movie *Glory*), the color-bearer fell. Before the flag touched the ground, Carney leaped forward to catch and advance it at the head of the attack. Although wounded three times, he proudly boasted after the battle that "the old flag never touched the ground."[38]

An Afro-Virginian woman warned federal authorities of the Confederacy's greatest secret weapon, the ironclad *Virginia* (*Merrimac*). Mary Louveste of Norfolk, an employee of the Gosport Navy Yard, where the *Virginia* was under construction, crossed Confederate lines and secretly journeyed to Washington for a private meeting with Secretary of the Navy Gideon Welles. She produced plans for the ship and described its condition and probable date of completion in detail. Louveste had spied for the federal government since the war's beginning, and because of her report Welles remained unruffled after the *Virginia* made its impressive debut at Hampton Roads in March 1862. Thanks to Louveste, Welles knew the Union's own *Monitor* could defeat the Confederate vessel. After the war he and other Union officials endorsed her pension application.[39]

Conclusion

Afro-Virginians were determined to secure recognition of their humanity, freedom, and citizenship after the war's end. In May 1865 Norfolk blacks held a meeting and resolved, "The rights and interests of the colored citizens of Virginia are more directly, immediately and deeply affected in the restoration of the State to the Federal Union than any other class of citizens. . . . We have peculiar claims to be heard in regard to the question of reconstruction, and that we cannot keep silent without dereliction of duty to ourselves, to our country, and to our God." In response to refusals by many slaveowners to give up their slaves and to political pressure from free blacks, Union military authorities issued a proclamation effective on May 26, 1865, that forever ended hereditary servitude in Virginia. When asked what blacks would do with their freedom, one former slave replied, "Our masters have always told us that we could not live without them, but [we] will show them that liberty makes men; that we can, and will be something."[40]

Against seemingly impossible odds, African Americans have survived and endured; theirs is an American heritage of fortitude and resilience. The Civil War, the past that endures, continues to influence American culture. "We are not makers of history," said the Reverend Dr. Martin Luther King, Jr., "We are made by history."[41] History is a nation's memory, but nations tend to ignore or forget the worst about themselves. Due to residual racism, the romanticization and sanitization of southern and Confederate history, and scholarly inertia, substantial evidence of African Americans' roles in the development of American civilization had until recently been concealed or overlooked.

No apology has ever been offered to African Americans for slavery, and this exceedingly profound cultural and national debt remains. During the war's 1960–65 centennial, black southerners' complaints about the glorification of the Confederacy during a time of segregation and white supremacy were silenced or relegated to the background. John Hope Franklin, the nation's preeminent African-American historian, criticized the huge expenditure of public money for national idolization of those who fought for slavery.[42]

The African-American experience in the United States is unlike that of other ethnic groups who came voluntarily. The mass relocation of Africans by force and their descendants' struggle for freedom and civil rights has compelled America to comply with its constitutional guarantees and recognize and protect the rights of all its citizens. Shortly after the war, Frederick Douglass prophetically warned that the future and survival of American democracy hinged on its treatment of African-American citizens: "If with the Negro was success in war, and without him failure, so in peace it will be found that the nation must fall or flourish with the Negro."[43]

Notes

1. Bruce Catton, *The American Heritage Picture History of the Civil War* (New York: American Heritage Publishing Company, 1960), 422–23; Ervin L. Jordan, Jr., *Black Confederates and Afro-Yankees in Civil War Virginia* (Charlottesville and London: University Press of Virginia, 1995), 269.

2. "Tribute strange, touching," *Richmond Times-Dispatch,* June 9, 1991; "Civil War soldier's remains lie in state," *Charlottesville Daily Progress,* June 9, 1991.

3. Calder Loth, ed., *Virginia Landmarks of Black History: Sites on the Virginia Landmarks Register and the National Register of Historic Places* (Charlottesville and London: University Press of Virginia, 1995), 79–81.

4. Patricia L. Faust, ed., *Historical Times Illustrated Encyclopedia of the Civil War* (New York: Harper and Row, 1986); Joyce Appleby, "Recovering America's Historic Diversity: Beyond Exceptionalism," *Journal of American History* 79 (September 1992): 428.

5. *The Index: A Weekly Journal of Politics, Literature, and News: Devoted to the Exposition of the Mutual Interests, Political and Commercial, of Great Britain and the Confederate States of America* (London), November 20, 1863, 58; Ethan Allen Andrews, *Slavery and the Domestic Slave-Trade in the United States* (Boston: Light and Stearns, 1836), 135–43; Frederic Bancroft, *Slave Trading in the Old South* (New York: Ungar, 1959), 91–93; Moncure Daniel Conway, *Testimonies Concerning Slavery* (London: Chapman and Hall, 1864), 19–26; James Barber, *Alexandria in the Civil War* (Lynchburg, Va.: H. E. Howard, 1988), 26, 63.

6. Silas and R. H. Omohundro Business Ledger, Silas and R. H. Omohundro Collection (#4122), Special Collections Department, University of Virginia Library, Charlottesville; Omohundro Business Records, "Money Paid out and Received, No. 1, 1851–1877," Silas Omohundro Papers, Library of Virginia, Richmond.

7. *American Missionary,* November 1861, 258.

8. Charles W. White, *The Hidden and the Forgotten: Contributions of Buckingham Blacks to American History* (Marceline, Mo.: Walsworth Press, 1985), 83–84.

9. Mary T. Hunley Diary, June 5, 1863, Southern Historical Collection, University of North Carolina, Chapel Hill (hereafter cited as SHC).

10. Washington Jackson Petition, Rockbridge Historical Society Collection, Leyburn Library, Washington and Lee University, Lexington, Va.

11. *Christian Observer*, February 7, 1861; Mary A. Livermore, *My Story of the War* (Hartford, Conn.: A. Worthington and Company, 1889), 259–62.

12. Catherine Barbara Broun Diary, December 27, 1863, 2:31, SHC; *Principia*, July 16, 1863; Francis Fedric, *Slave Life in Virginia and Kentucky* (London: Wertheim, Macintosh, and Hunt, 1863), 11.

13. Marguerite du Pont Lee, *Virginia Ghosts*, rev. ed. (Berryville, Va.: Virginia Book Company, 1966), 237–38.

14. *Code of Virginia, Including Legislation to the Year 1860*, 2d ed. (Richmond, Va.: Ritchie, Dunnavant, and Company, 1860), 815–17, 847–49; "Condemned Slaves, Transported" folders, 1861, 1862, 1865, Auditor of Public Accounts: Condemned Blacks Executed or Transported, 1783–1865, entry 756, box 1792, RG 48.756, Library of Virginia.

15. Booker T. Washington, *The Story of My Life and Work* (Toronto, Ont.: J. L. Nichols and Company, 1900), 30, 32.

16. Austin Steward, *Twenty-two Years a Slave, and Forty Years a Freeman* (Rochester, N.Y.: William Alling, 1857), 15; George Ryley Scott, *The History of Torture throughout the Ages* (London: Torchstream Books, 1954), 196; Charles L. Perdue, Jr., Thomas E. Barden, and Robert K. Phillips, eds., *Weevils in the Wheat: Interviews with Virginia Ex-Slaves* (Charlottesville: University Press of Virginia, 1976), 43–44.

17. *Richmond Examiner*, June 30, 1864; *Daily Richmond Examiner*, July 1, 1864.

18. *Alexandria Gazette*, March 14, 1861; *The Liberator* (Boston), October 24, 1862.

19. Robert E. Lee: Custis Executor Document, Eleanor S. Brockenbrough Library, Museum of the Confederacy, Richmond, Va.

20. Thomas J. Wertenbaker, *Norfolk: Historic Southern Port*, 2d ed., ed. Marvin W. Schlegel (Durham, N.C.: Duke University Press, 1962), 220–21.

21. Jacob Hoke, *The Great Invasion of 1863, or General Lee in Pennsylvania* (Dayton, Ohio: W. J. Shuey, 1887), 96, 108; Albertus McCreary, "Gettysburg: A Boy's Experience of the Battle," *McClure's Magazine* 33 (July 1909): 250. To Confederate soldiers who invaded the North, any African American was a slave. Some Pennsylvania free blacks were rescued by Union troops after Gettysburg (U.S. War Department, *The War of the Rebellion: A*

Compilation of the Official Records of the Union and Confederate Armies [Washington, D.C.: Government Printing Office, 1880–1901], ser. 1, vol. 27, pt. 1, pp. 970–71).

22. Eleanor P. Cross and Charles B. Cross, Jr., eds., *Glencoe Diary: The War-Time Journal of Elizabeth Curtis Wallace* (Chesapeake, Va.: Norfolk County Historical Society, 1968), 24; *Richmond Enquirer,* October 29, 1862.

23. Harrison to A. Lincoln, July 28, 1862, Records of the Office of the Secretary of War, RG 107, microfilm 494, roll 1, National Archives, Washington, D.C.; Ervin L. Jordan, Jr., "Sleeping with the Enemy: Sex, Black Women, and the Civil War," *Western Journal of Black Studies* 18 (Summer 1994): 58.

24. *National Anti-Slavery Standard,* July 23, 1864.

25. Henry L. Estabrooks, *Adrift in Dixie* (New York: Carleton, 1866), 122–23, 174–76.

26. House Committee on War Claims, *Summary Reports of the Commissioners of Claims* (Washington, D.C.: Government Printing Office, 1871–80), 2:253.

27. *Richmond Daily Examiner,* March 15, 1865; Ervin L. Jordan, Jr., *Charlottesville and the University of Virginia in the Civil War* (Lynchburg, Va.: H. E. Howard, 1988), 40; House Committee on War Claims, *Summary Reports,* 3:143.

28. Fedric, *Slave Life,* 10; Jordan, "Sleeping," 59–60.

29. *American Missionary,* April 1864, 93.

30. Elizabeth Keckley, *Behind the Scenes, or Thirty Years a Slave and Four Years in the White House* (New York: Oxford University Press, 1988), xxvii–xxxvi.

31. Afro-Confederates increasingly are attracting scholarly attention. See index entry "Afro-Confederates" in Jordan, *Black Confederates,* 405; Richard Rollins, ed., *Black Southerners in Gray: Essays on Afro-Americans in Confederate Armies* (Murfreesboro, Tenn.: Southern Heritage Press, 1994); *Journal of Confederate History,* vols. 11, 14; Charles Kelly Barrow, J. H. Segars, and R. B. Rosenburg, eds., *Forgotten Confederates: An Anthology about Black Southerners* (Atlanta: Southern Heritage Press, 1995).

32. *American Missionary,* October 1861, 245; *Atlantic Monthly,* November 1861, 638.

33. *Douglass' Monthly,* February 1862, 598; *Harper's Weekly,* May 10, 1862.

34. Joseph T. Wilson, *The Black Phalanx* (Hartford, Conn.: American Publishing Company, 1888), 498.

35. Lewis H. Steiner, *Report of Lewis H. Steiner, M.D., Inspector of the Sanitary Commission, Containing a Diary* (New York: Anson D. F. Randolph, 1862), 20; *New York Herald,* July 11, 1863.

36. "Bill to Increase the Military Force of the Confederate States" (House), February 10, 1865; "Bill to Provide for Raising 200,000 Negro Troops" (Senate), February 10, 1865; and "Amendment Proposed by the Committee on Military Affairs to the Bill (Senate 190) to Provide for Raising 200,000 Negro Troops," February 13, 1865, *Journal of the Congress of the Confederate States of America, 1861–1865* (Washington, D.C.: U.S. Government Publications Office, 1904–5) (U.S. Serials Set, vols. 4610–16), 7:562, 4:543, 4:550.

37. H. C. Scott to Colonel Scott Shipp, March 16, 1865, Confederate Information Index, Slaves, entry 453, RG 109, National Archives, Washington, D.C.; *Watchman* (New York), April 1866; R. A. Brock, "Paroles of the Army of Northern Virginia," *Southern Historical Society Papers* 15 (1887): 45, 63, 487.

38. Joseph B. Mitchell, *Badge of Gallantry* (New York: Macmillan, 1968), 132–34; *The Congressional Medal of Honor* (Forest Ranch, Calif.: Sharp and Dunnigan Publications, 1984), 739.

39. Thomas C. Parramore, Peter C. Stewart, and Tommy L. Bogger, *Norfolk: The First Four Centuries* (Charlottesville and London: University Press of Virginia, 1994), 203.

40. *Equal Suffrage: Address from the Colored Citizens of Norfolk, Va., to the People of the United States. Also an Account of the Agitation among the Colored People of Virginia for Equal Rights* (New Bedford, Mass.: 1865; rpt. Wilmington, Del.: Scholarly Resources, 1970?), 23–26.

41. Martin Luther King, Jr., as quoted in Dorothy Winbush Riley, ed., *My Soul Looks Back, 'Less I Forget: A Collection of Quotations by People of Color* (New York: HarperCollins, 1993), 190.

42. John Hope Franklin, "A Century of Civil War Observance," *Journal of Negro History* 47 (April 1962): 103–4, 106–7.

43. Frederick Douglass, "Reconstruction," *Atlantic Monthly*, December 1866, 761–65.

Contributors

GARY W. GALLAGHER is professor of history at the University of Virginia. He holds M.A. and Ph.D. degrees from the University of Texas and has written and edited numerous books relating to the Civil War, including *Fighting for the Confederacy: The Personal Recollections of General Edward Porter Alexander* (1989), *Jubal A. Early, the Lost Cause, and Civil War History: A Persistent Legacy* (1995), *The Confederate War* (1997), and *Lee and His Generals in War and Memory* (1998).

JOSEPH T. GLATTHAAR is professor of history at the University of Houston. He received an M.A. from Rice University and a Ph.D. from the University of Wisconsin-Madison and has published *The March to the Sea and Beyond: Sherman's Troops in the Savannah and Carolinas Campaigns* (1985), *Forged in Battle: The Civil War Alliance of Black Soldiers and White Officers* (1990), and *Partners in Command: The Relationships between Leaders in the Civil War* (1994).

ERVIN L. JORDAN, JR., holds an M.A. from Old Dominion University and specializes in Civil War and African-American history. He serves as curator of technical services and is an associate professor at the University of Virginia Library. He has published two books, *Charlottesville and the University of Virginia in the Civil War* (1988) and *Black Confederates and Afro-Yankees in Civil War Virginia* (1995), and co-authored a third, *19th Virginia Infantry* (1987).

MARK E. NEELY, JR., is the John Francis Bannon Professor of History and American Studies at St. Louis University and holds a Ph.D. from Yale University. His *The Fate of Liberty: Abraham Lincoln and Civil Liberties* (1991) won the Pulitzer Prize for history. Neely's other works include *The Last Best Hope of Earth: Abraham Lincoln and the Promise of America* (1993) and *Mine Eyes Have Seen the Glory: The Civil War in Art* (1993, co-authored with Harold Holzer).

ALAN T. NOLAN, a graduate of Harvard Law School, is an Indianapolis attorney. He has written two historical books, *The Iron Brigade: A Military History* (1961) and *Lee Considered: General Robert E. Lee and Civil War History* (1991), as well as a novel, *As Sounding Brass*.

JAMES I. ROBERTSON, JR., holds a Ph.D. from Emory University and a Litt.D. from Randolph-Macon College and is the Alumni Distinguished Professor in History at Virginia Polytechnic Institute and State University. He is the author of numerous works, including *General A. P. Hill: The Story of a Confederate Warrior* (1987); *Soldiers Blue and Gray* (1988), a Pulitzer Prize nominee; *Civil War! America Becomes One Nation* (1992); and *Stonewall Jackson, the Man, the Soldier, the Legend* (1997).

JOHN Y. SIMON holds a Ph.D. from Harvard University and is professor of history at Southern Illinois University. Since 1962 he has served as editor of the *Papers of Ulysses S. Grant*, twenty-two volumes of which have been published since 1967. A prolific writer and recipient of numerous awards, Simon is a founder and a past president of the Association for Documentary Editing.

MICHAEL E. STEVENS is State Historian of Wisconsin at the State Historical Society of Wisconsin. He holds M.A. and Ph.D. degrees from the University of Wisconsin-Madison. His most recent book is *As If It Were Glory: Robert Beecham's Civil War, from the Iron Brigade to the Black Regiments* (1998).

Index

NEW PERSPECTIVES ON THE CIVIL WAR
is set in Fournier, a historical recutting of the
eighteenth-century French typeface designed by
Pierre-Simon Fournier. Similar in period and
feel to the English faces Baskerville and Bell,
Fournier is a transitional face that straddles the
Neoclassical and Modern periods in typeface
design. Indeed, Fournier's influence are clearly
evident in the revolutionary "modern" faces
designed by Giambattista Bodoni. Reintroduced
to a twentieth-century audience in 1925 by
Stanley Morison and the Monotype Corporation,
Fournier retains much of the elegance and
distinction of the earlier French version.

Design by Gregory M. Britton